Kingdom and Country is an unflinch
In confronting the beast that is Chr
authors do so with great wisdom, ho......., ...
Drawing on crucial concepts like the nature of allegiance,
the myths of our country's origin, and the importance of the
pulpit in national and Kingdom life, this book will be a great
source of wisdom and a companion on the journey to faithful
witness and Kingdom living.

LISA RODRIGUEZ-WATSON, national director of Missio Alliance

While many seek to collapse Kingdom and country into
one or remove concern for country from those dedicated
to Kingdom, this new work edited by Angie Ward seeks to
clarify what is at stake in the discourse today about Christian
nationalism. In this integrative work, authors take theological
frameworks as the foundation for practical engagement in
our world. Is polarization our fundamental problem, or is it
injustice? We are divided, yes, but is all division unfaithful?
And how do we discern what makes for peace? What is
needed to reclaim our Christian identity and vocation from
nationalistic narratives in order to bear witness to God's
Kingdom in a country coming apart at the seams? *Kingdom
and Country* calls and equips the church to discern well
how to embody a redemptive presence in the places where
rectification and reconciliation are needed most.

REV. MATT TEBBE, cofounder of Gravity Leadership, copastor at
The Table, and coauthor of *Having the Mind of Christ: Eight Axioms to
Cultivate a Robust Faith*

Angie Ward has assembled a group of diverse, experienced, and influential contributors who articulate the central issues in our nation's divides. Many Christians today have forgotten that this world is not our home. We have placed our hope not in Jesus but in politics, powers, and principalities. As you read this book, you will be reminded and challenged that we live not just for this temporal reality; we live purposefully now to advance the Kingdom of God.

MATTHEW D. KIM, George F. Bennett professor of preaching and practical theology at Gordon-Conwell Theological Seminary, author of *Preaching to People in Pain*, and coauthor of *Preaching to a Divided Nation*

This may be the most critical conversation for the American church right now. Unflinching and full of love, Dr. Ward and her team address the elephants in our room with wisdom, nuance, and much-needed biblical truth. Every pastor should read this book!

ROB BRENDLE, pastor, author of *In the Meantime: The Practice of Proactive Waiting*

Angie Ward has gathered an impressive group of Christian leaders to help us understand what it means to be a citizen of the United States and a disciple of Jesus Christ. If you seek a renewal of spiritual community amid the political divisiveness that has divided the church in the past decade, this is a good place to start.

JOHN FEA, distinguished professor of history at Messiah University, author of *Was America Founded as a Christian Nation?: A Historical Introduction*

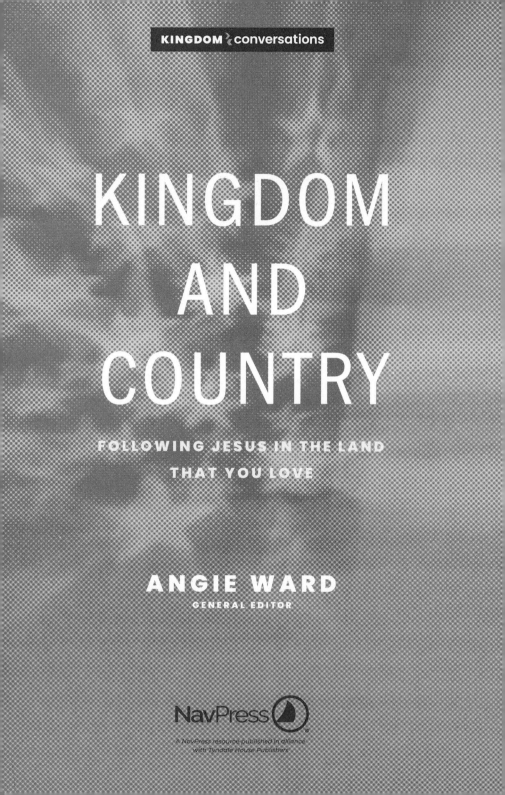

KINGDOM conversations

KINGDOM AND COUNTRY

FOLLOWING JESUS IN THE LAND THAT YOU LOVE

ANGIE WARD
GENERAL EDITOR

NavPress

A NavPress resource published in alliance
with Tyndale House Publishers

NavPress ◐

NavPress is the publishing ministry of The Navigators, an international Christian organization and leader in personal spiritual development. NavPress is committed to helping people grow spiritually and enjoy lives of meaning and hope through personal and group resources that are biblically rooted, culturally relevant, and highly practical.

For more information, visit NavPress.com.

CONTENTS

INTRODUCTION

"The next book in the Kingdom Conversations series will be *Kingdom and Country*," I'd explain. The responses became predictable—and, I'll admit, mildly amusing.

An arched brow. A bemused smirk. A slight tilt of the head, not unlike the look my dog gives me when he thinks I'm crazy.

"Kingdom and country. Really?!"

"Ooh. Wow."

"That will be . . . *interesting*."

Perhaps you had the same response when you picked up this book. You are wondering what it will say, where you will agree or disagree, whether it might make you angry. (*Caveat lector:* It might.)

So why would we dare to publish a book about Christian nationalism? Why poke the bear? Why enter where angels seemingly fear to tread?

Either because we are completely foolish, or because a book like this is absolutely necessary for those of us who claim to be followers of Christ at this moment in history. I'd suggest it's the latter, but maybe it's a little of both. Read it and decide for yourself.

The last US presidential election cycle was perhaps the most polarized—and divisive—in history. Of course, we said that about the election before that. And the one before that. Which means that the next one will be even worse than the last one. And this is not just happening in the United States. Our world is fracturing along multiple fault lines. The rifts are growing deeper. We've gone beyond name-calling to questioning character and Christian integrity.

What can we do to stop the madness?

Let's start by calling out the elephant—wait, bad political metaphor—let's name the things that are dividing us. Let's look together at Scripture, theology, history, and Jesus' example, and at what they have to say to us today. And let's get personal—as in, looking at ourselves, examining our temptations to participate in partisanship and to pursue power, and how these affect the trajectory of our hearts and the power of our witness.

In keeping with the spirit and tone of the Kingdom Conversations series, when curating the group of contributors for this book, we looked for women and men who were first and foremost disciples of Christ, servants of the King of kings.

We sought authors, teachers, and pastors who balanced boldness with humility. And we wanted voices who could speak from deep wells of expertise and personal experience.

They went above and beyond our wildest hopes. The result is a thought-provoking—and eyebrow-raising, head-tilting, perhaps even gut-punching, yet ever-gracious—collective challenge to consider how we as Christians can and must follow Jesus in the land that we love.

Rod Wilson begins by asking if we can even talk about charged topics, using the lens of a true-to-life small group to help us see why these conversations are so challenging. Next, Karen Wilk outlines a compelling theology of the Kingdom of God, painting a powerful picture of the Kingdom near, here, and now.

Ryan Tafilowski follows with an overview of the church's mixed relationship to worldly powers and principalities over the course of history. What can we learn from those who have gone before? In a similar vein, Derek Vreeland reminds us, as the modern people of God, of the rhythms of the ancient people of God—the people of Israel—as they navigated the tensions of living under human governance yet under God's ultimate authority.

Sean Palmer makes it more personal, challenging our understanding and declarations of allegiance. Michelle Reyes then explores the concept of national narratives, and how we are shaped by the mythology and ethos of where we grew up. Tina Boesch—no stranger to life as a foreigner—delves into what it means to live as dual citizens of heaven and earth. And Alejandro Mandes calls us to love those we classify as "other" as our brothers and sisters, fellow image-bearers of God.

Juliet Liu then takes the discussion into the local church. What should a gospel politic look like for pastors and parishioners? Finally, Mandy Smith leads us in a liturgy of humility and a pledge of Kingdom citizenship.

I invite you to join your fellow Kingdom sojourners on this road toward hope and healing.

Angie Ward
GENERAL EDITOR

1

CAN WE HAVE
A CONVERSATION?

Rod Wilson

IT HAS BEEN A SAD SEASON in the life of the Brownlee Home Group at Thornbury Community Church.

Before the US presidential primaries of 2016, members enjoyed each other's company, discussed biblical issues thoughtfully, and appreciated the shared support. But in recent years, they have stopped meeting regularly. Many of them do not speak to each other, and respectful dialogue between them has ceased.

Some see Fred's anger as a significant contributor to the fracture. As their conversations have drifted into the political realm, he has become increasingly enraged. For him, Christians should have nothing to do with politics. God's

Kingdom is separate and distinct and has nothing to do with what is happening in Washington.

Sharlene's angst has resulted in some group members feeling like they cannot share anymore. Immigration preoccupies Sharlene, and she fears that the liberal left will create a country of lawlessness. Every discussion ends up at immigration for Sharlene, and her anxiety has stifled conversation.

The mere mention of Donald Trump's name triggers Graham. Throughout the 2016 and 2020 elections, his rants caused group members to be concerned for his health. They had hoped that the election of Joe Biden would bring an end to Graham's preoccupation, but it became easier to avoid attending the group than listen to his endless diatribes.

Letisha has strong feelings about pastors speaking directly and at length about political matters. Her opinion is that the pulpit is the place to be clear about the issues and the candidates during election time. While some participants agreed with her perspective, her obsession with the topic wearied them.

Fred's anger, Sharlene's angst, Graham's triggers, and Letisha's opinions all converged to create an environment in which conversation became nearly impossible. Being Christians with a shared love for the Lord did not seem to provide an adequate foundation for the Brownlee Home Group to engage in fruitful dialogue despite their political differences.

Sound familiar?

We live in a politicized time. And make no mistake:

Political issues matter. They are tied to our deepest beliefs and values. Political decisions have the potential to affect so much of our lives. We wonder: *Can we still be ourselves? Will we be able to engage in our usual activities, or will those be taken away from us? Might political decisions influence what we have or do not have?* When there is a chance that our ways of being, doing, and having might be changed, it is no wonder that we experience a strong emotional response.

Yet as Christians we are called—even commanded—to live in community with others and to love others, even when we do not share the same values or perspectives. How can we do this when we can't even talk to one another?

As we embark on a conversation about Kingdom and country, let's start with the example of Jesus and then revisit the Brownlee Home Group with principles that can help us learn how to engage in honest and loving dialogue.

Jesus Chose Conversation

John 4 tells the story of Jesus with the Samaritan woman at the well. It's a familiar passage: On a journey from Judea to Galilee, Jesus chose to travel through the region of Samaria, where he stopped at a well in the town of Sychar. While resting there in the heat of midday, he interacted with a Samaritan woman who had come to draw water.

There were multiple reasons why Jesus and the woman shouldn't even have talked. It was unthinkable for Jesus, a Jewish male, to talk publicly to a Samaritan woman in the middle of the day. Even though going through Samaria was the shortest route to get from Jerusalem to Galilee, any self-respecting Jew knew that doing so would lead to defilement through contact with an ethnic group that didn't share their values, participated in syncretistic worship, and taught that Mount Gerizim (not Jerusalem) was the proper place to worship. It might have made for a longer walk, but Jews were supposed to go around Samaria. The guideline was clear: Don't associate with people who don't share your socio-political-religious convictions.

And all this was only the context. The woman herself had significant challenges from her marriages and sexual history. A righteous rabbi in dialogue with a woman of questionable character? It was unthinkable to those in Jesus' day.

How did Jesus navigate this situation? Through a conversation.

He could have (and by cultural and religious dictates *should* have) avoided associating with her. Maybe he could have preached, lectured, or taught her, from a distance. Possibly a group could have gathered, and he could have presented a seminar. But Jesus chose to give her the dignity of interaction, the gift of a listening ear, the context of conversation to speak truth. Not only did the woman turn toward life but she became an evangelist, leading many to Christ and causing the Samaritans to invite Jesus to stay longer.

This is only one example of many in Scripture where Jesus chose conversation, not disengagement or diatribe. Think of his interactions with the crippled beggar, the rich young ruler, tax collectors and sinners, even the Pharisees and those who wanted to kill him. What principles can guide us to engage similarly in Christlike conversation about difficult topics?

Balance the Truth with the Way

When people speak of a "Christian" viewpoint on politics, they are usually referencing what they view as the truth, not the nature of the conversation itself. They purport to have a theological conviction or biblical passage that forms the basis of their belief yet often miss the significance of the method of communication. But as Eugene Peterson writes:

> The Jesus way wedded to the Jesus truth brings about the Jesus life. We can't proclaim the Jesus truth but do it any old way we like. Nor can we follow the Jesus way without speaking the Jesus truth.
>
> But Jesus as the truth gets far more attention than Jesus as the way. . . . We cannot skip the way of Jesus in our hurry to get the truth of Jesus.[1]

Quality conversations should balance *conviction* with *curiosity*. They can be a venue for the expression of conviction, where we can state our views, provide a rationale, use understandable language, and do so respectfully. But they should also be characterized by curiosity in our willingness to be fully present, listen with vigilance, postpone evaluation, and seek understanding. Life will only be evident if truth is believed and practiced in a way that is congruous with that truth.

In the Brownlee Home Group, it was clear to everyone that Letisha had strong opinions on what pastors should do during the lead-up to an election. The problem was that despite her claims, there is no biblical directive that would lead everyone else to such a conclusion. Furthermore, her conclusiveness on her conclusions made any form of conversation a door closer.

Three Latin words will help us lay a foundation for reflecting on quality interaction.

Controversia, from which we get our word *controversial*, means "turned in an opposite direction" or "turned against" something.[2]

Contentionem, the source of our word *contentious*, is "a vigorous struggling, a contest, a fight."[3]

Conversari, like *conversation*, describes associating with others.

People have diverse beliefs, hold discrepant ethical convictions, and vote for different parties. Democracy, by its very nature, allows for these realities. The question is how we should deal with these dissimilar approaches. Do we adopt a contentious spirit, where we fight and scuffle as if we are in a battle with our fellow citizens? Or do we associate with people, engage in conversation, and participate in respectful dialogue?

Practicing the latter reflects an understanding that all people are fallen image-bearers, made of strength and struggle, gifts and grime. Not just those who are like me and share my political leanings, but *all* people. Disrespecting someone by not engaging in conversation with them is a loud statement on what we think of their Maker (Proverbs 14:31; 17:5; James 3:9-10).

With a commitment to conversation and associating with others, our mode of engagement becomes clearer. While diatribe and debate may have their place in human interaction, discourse and dialogue allow for more cooperative interchange.[4] If Letisha could deliver substantive information from history through a discourse that allowed others to understand the source of her opinions, that would ease the tension in the group. Better yet, if she allowed for two-way, cooperative dialogue where information was exchanged both ways, group conversations on what pastors should do during elections would be much less contentious.

Manage Our Emotions

Because God created us in his image, it is not a surprise that we experience and express emotions. Our capacity to feel is one of the ways we mirror our Creator. But poorly managed emotions can shut down the conversational ideal presented by Jesus. When subjects are controversial and contentious, interaction can become unproductive and dialogue muted.

The apostle Paul exhorts Christians, "If it is possible, as far as it depends on you, live at peace with everyone" (Romans 12:18). We cannot control what others think or believe, or how they respond to our words. We can only manage our own emotions and behaviors, helping to create an environment that is safe for everyone to participate.

Managing Anger

It wouldn't be appropriate for the other members of the Brownlee Home Group to criticize Fred because he feels anger. Some social scientists argue that there are six primary emotions—love, joy, surprise, anger, sadness, and fear.[5] Fred's rage reflects his humanity. But is his anger Christian, loving, and a conversation facilitator? One of the best ways to answer this question is to explore the Greek text of the New Testament. Its clarity and specificity shine a light on the various facets of anger.

The biblical text is direct in describing what happened when the disciples rebuked the people bringing children to have Jesus touch them: "When Jesus saw this, he was indignant" (Mark 10:14). The Greek word translated "was indignant" (*aganakteō*) communicates a sense of irritation, grief, and annoyance at what someone else has done, particularly if it is unjust. The lack of compassion demonstrated by the disciples irritated Jesus, for a good reason. It wasn't a petty issue that bothered him, but something that violated the clear teaching of the gospel that children and other marginalized groups should be treated with respect and offered hospitality.[6]

Earlier in Mark's Gospel, Jesus was going to heal a man with a shriveled hand, but the religious people reminded him that this should not happen on the Sabbath. Again, the biblical text is clear on Jesus' anger: "He looked around at them in anger . . . deeply distressed at their stubborn hearts" (Mark 3:5). Disturbed by the stubbornness of people who should know better, Jesus expressed anger—this time the word used is *orgē* (pronounced *or-gay*), an emotion that indicates a settled judgment.

Jesus' anger did not contain personal animosity or vengeance as he confronted the offense. Paul's reminder in Ephesians 4:31—"Get rid of all . . . anger [*orgē*]"—as well as his caution in Ephesians 4:26—"In your anger [*orgizō*] do not sin"—show us that to experience frustration and distress with someone is not inherently sinful. But it will move this way if we are not mindful of the need for righteous expression.

While acknowledging irritation and settled judgment, the Bible also speaks of exasperation, or *parorgismos*: a slow, smoldering irritation that is not a full-blown rage but is part of the anger repertoire. Paul says, "Do not let the sun go down while you are still angry [*parorgismos*], and do not give the devil a foothold" (Ephesians 4:26-27). It is not that we should never go to bed angry. But if we cultivate exasperation over time, we can expect this to be an invitation to the devil to do his work. Being occasionally irritated is both appropriate and human, but excessively nurturing this feeling is dangerous.

While *parorgismos* is a sort of exasperation, *thymos* is an all-encompassing body rage and temper. It is an emotion that exhibits no control or self-discipline but lashes out at the other person in a completely inappropriate way. Like the striking of a match, this anger flares up with a boiling, turbulent commotion before it simmers down. Many of us have experienced this emotion, the cruel, demeaning attitude that lacks love and respect. Paul indicates that we are to "get rid of all . . . rage [*thymos*]" (Ephesians 4:31). The Bible never condones unbridled temper or uncontrolled rage.

Fred feels strongly about the relationship of Christianity and politics, but he has not learned the grace of thoughtful indignation or settled judgment. Instead, he has opted for long-held exasperation with large doses of rage. Whatever the merits of his position may be, his mode of expression is neither Christian nor facilitative of conversation.[7]

Managing Angst

Meanwhile, when group members talked about Sharlene's preoccupation with immigration policies and her constant references to crimes committed by noncitizens, they used words like *anxiety*, *fear*, and *angst*. No one was trying to give a precise technical definition. They knew that she was obsessed with the topic. Every discussion moved in that direction, with high-strung emotion and normal conversation ground to a halt.

Fear is a response to a specific threat that is real or imagined. That is why phrases like "fear of flying," "fear of public speaking," or "fear of snakes" indicate a sense of danger. Anxiety, in contrast, is more of a free-floating emotion of unease and nervousness. Being anxious about the stock market or our child's vocational choice is usually more general and lacks a particular focus. Angst may be best described as an inner emotional turmoil that includes apprehension and concern with threads of fear and anxiety.[8]

These various windows into emotion are all characterized by three things:

- questions of *What if . . . ?*;
- a feeling of loss of control; and
- lack of clarity on the consequences of decisions.

When Sharlene thinks about immigration, she immediately completes the *What if . . . ?* phrase with *all the criminals arrive*, or *we lose our founding principles as a country*, or *our Christian faith gets marginalized*. In previous years she felt comfortable with her place in the culture, but now Sharlene feels out of control. She lacks confidence, control, and clarity—and she cannot do anything about it.

In the group, Sharlene gets amped up as if she has an excessive electrical charge. Little does she realize the impact of this behavior on the group. When an individual does not steward their angst well in a group context, several things ensue. There is less likelihood of dissent and a propensity to keep quiet, along with a decrease in questioning and challenging because topics seem threatening. Indecisiveness overcomes the group, and frustration permeates the ethos. Conversation is muted, and the angst becomes contagious.[9]

In the North American context, electrical voltage comes into our homes and offices at 120 volts. Most of our cell phones require 5 volts to function effectively. Within the charger, there is a small transformer that converts the 120 volts to 5 volts. Otherwise, the phone would burn up. In electrical terms, this is a step-down process, whereby extreme power is taken down to aid the proper functioning of the cell phone.

Like the rest of us, Sharlene is exposed to a massive amount of socio-cultural and political information through various media. This powerful communication is loud, excessive, and fear-facilitating. If this power is not stepped down, it quickly amps us up and becomes a barrier to good conversation. Sharlene comes to the group wired, bringing 120 volts into the room, and now everyone is fried. How can she bring down the voltage?

Sharlene may need to put parameters around how much news she consumes every day. Building in some quiet, reflective prayer after hearing reports on immigration will put the picture in the right frame. Even a time of silence before small group, with an internal commitment to stay with the night's topic, will provide essential management.

Because angst can reflect fear, fear can mask threats, and threats can be deeply personal, Sharlene may also need to do some inner work. What is the source of her fear? Why is immigration so threatening? Finally, she may need to immerse herself in the biblical narrative. The trajectory from fear to faith is not a simple flip of the switch, where we move from the former to the latter. It is an ongoing journey where we bring our what-ifs to the only one who knows the rest of the sentence. It is a daily commitment where we admit that only the Creator, not the created, is in control. It is a life of faith where we do not always see the consequences of human decisions.

Recognize the Effects of Our Own Story

God has designed each of us with a sophisticated system to help us process information, including what are commonly known as "triggers." As you are reading this book, various parts of your brain are engaged. The thalamus is collecting and organizing all the information so two central areas of the brain can comprehend it. The amygdala or limbic system is the feeling brain, where various emotions are rooted and experienced. The thinking brain is the neocortex or prefrontal lobe system, where information is taken in and understood. Even as you read this paragraph, your brain organizes these various definitions, you experience emotion, and your comprehension is enhanced.

The hippocampus is closely linked to the amygdala and is the part of the brain that relates to memory. In other words, the emotions that flare up in the amygdala can be traced to historical memories. If you failed a neuroscience course as an undergraduate, you might be in fight-or-flight mode at this very moment! On the other hand, if you know little about the brain that God put inside you, you may be experiencing feelings of interest and curiosity. The amygdala and hippocampus are doing their job. Triggers are part of who we are.

As the amygdala and neocortex receive and process what

has been taken in by the thalamus, information is sent to the autonomic nervous system. Depending on the reaction, the body responds through changes in blood pressure, body temperature, pulse rate, and the like. A red face, quick breathing, and strong body movements may reflect a fight response. A flight reaction may show up in someone looking away or physically leaving the room. In addition, our memories of past events inform our thinking and feeling in the present moment, and that response shows up in bodily reactions when specific incidents occur or particular things are said. Typically, that leads to one of four responses: fight, flight, freeze, or fawn. This is not just psychological mumbo jumbo. It is God's created design.[10]

Graham's reaction to Donald Trump was a real puzzle to the rest of the Brownlee Home Group. They landed on the trigger explanation because that was the best way to describe what happened. Even if somebody just mentioned Trump's name in passing, you could see Graham breathe more quickly, tense his body, and then unleash a seething outburst. Discussion quickly ceased.

Graham grew up in poverty, and economic and interpersonal deprivation characterized his formative years. He defined himself as "less than" and "not enough." Gripped by shame, Graham always felt something was wrong with him, particularly in contrast to those who had money. His parents often talked about the "filthy rich" as the antithesis to their family. People with money, especially a lot of it, were the enemy and a threat. Around the dinner table, Graham's parents often held the wealthy responsible for their poverty.

For Graham, Donald Trump was the exemplar of all that his family was not. While he did not know all the details of Trump's life, he knew one thing: It was rich people like him who made poor people feel worth less than them. Whether that narrative was true didn't matter. Graham's hippocampus was full of stories, his amygdala was firing at lightning speed, and his body was impacted significantly. His previous experience led him to feel belittled or neglected, which created a feeling of insecurity. He responded emotionally by putting up his fists and throwing the first punch.

Given Graham's backstory and the nature of triggers, it would be futile for the Home Group to simply tell him to stop getting upset at the mention of Trump's name. The path forward will require everyone's participation. Graham would benefit from examining his reaction and where it comes from. For many people, triggers based on memories are unconscious and require patient exploration. Meanwhile, the other members of the Home Group can continue to reassure Graham of their love for him and their commitment to walking together. The best response to triggers is not argument but safety.

An Invitation

You are about to enter a conversation with my fellow authors as they deal with politically charged subjects that have the potential to fracture and divide. In subsequent weeks and months, you will no doubt have continued opportunities to engage others on these matters in your own relationships. Fred, Sharlene, Graham, and Letisha are like all of us. How we recognize and manage our opinions, emotions, and triggers will significantly influence our ability to facilitate and participate in Christlike conversation. Let us choose the Jesus way, so our conversations with others are respectful and compassionate, infused with conviction and curiosity.

2

THE KINGDOM
OF GOD IS HERE

Karen Wilk

A FRIEND OF MINE TELLS THE STORY of having to do street evangelism for a course he was taking at a Christian college a number of years ago. One had to "win" *x* number of souls to receive a passing grade. Regarding one attempt to present the gospel, he recalls this response: "You don't care about me. You just care about when I die." It made him wonder if the Good News was really good if it was simply about a ticket to God's Kingdom when you die. Dallas Willard calls this "barcode Christianity" by which we "swipe" our "decision" through the "great scanner in the sky" to guarantee our passage into the Kingdom of Heaven.[1] But Jesus didn't say, "Go and give out barcodes to heaven." It's not just a swipe! He said, "Go and make disciples." He said, "Follow me." And as Scot McKnight explains, "The only way we can follow him is to take up his kingdom vision and let it shape everything we do."[2]

Which leads to the question: What is his Kingdom vision? Surely, it's more than this once-popular brand of Christianity. In fact, when we pay attention to Jesus' announcement of the good news, we understand that it's the good news that the Kingdom of God is *near, here and now!* The phrase *Kingdom of God* (or Matthew's equivalent, the *Kingdom of Heaven*) "appears 122 times in the first three gospels—most of the time (92) on the lips of Jesus himself"[3] and rarely in reference to life after death.

When we reduce the Kingdom to life after death, not only can the good news *not* be good news to those struggling with daily life here and now ("You don't care about me") but God's people are excused from the call to follow and become more and more like Jesus—loving God, neighbor, enemy, and all of creation! After all, if the afterlife is what it's all about, then life on earth is just a waiting game. Why bother worrying about climate change or be concerned about social justice? And if I already have a "ticket to go," does it really matter how I behave? Our actions on earth become a moot point, so much so that some, including those in leadership, have justified (at least in their own minds) all sorts of immoral and unethical behaviors. Such actions and inactions have clearly distorted what it means to be a Jesus follower and detrimentally affected not only personal lives and local communities but our global witness.

Might it be time for us to pause—no, actually, to hammer the brakes, check the GPS, reorient, and set a new/ancient direction—in response to Jesus' primary proclamation: "The Kingdom of God *is near!*"? For when we turn to the Scriptures, there is little room for doubt that there is more to God's Kingdom than life in the hereafter.

The Kingdom Is Here—Says Who?

The biblical account informs us throughout that the universe and everything in it is God's Kingdom:

- "The LORD sits enthroned over the flood; the LORD is enthroned as King forever" (Psalm 29:10, see also Psalm 9:7).
- "For God is the king of all the earth" (Psalm 47:7).
- "O LORD the God of Israel, who are enthroned above the cherubim, you are God, you alone, of all the kingdoms of the earth; you have made heaven and earth" (2 Kings 19:15, NRSV).[4]

The Creator who made all things, including you and me, is the Lord of heaven and earth (see, e.g., Psalm 24:1; 1 Corinthians 10:26). "Who can fathom [it]?" exclaims the prophet Isaiah (Isaiah 40). God is sovereign over wind and waves, wombs and wanderers, those who know him and those who are yet to. Ezekiel is reminded of God's immanent dominion through a vision that he receives in foreign Babylon of all places (Ezekiel 1–2), the same exilic place where Jeremiah also declares that God is at work (Jeremiah 29). Jonah, too, discovers that God is reigning in countries beyond his sphere such that even sinful Ninevites are invited to recognize and be a part of his Kingdom (Jonah 3).[5] Prophets, priests and kings, peasants, servants, and even donkeys reveal that all things, heavens above and earth below, little sparrows and common lilies, all are under God's loving rule:

> Yours, O Lord, are the greatness, the power, the glory, the victory, and the majesty; for all that is in the heavens and on the earth is yours; yours is the kingdom, O Lord, and you are exalted as head above all.
>
> I CHRONICLES 29:11, NRSV

Old Testament writers keep telling us this, pointing to it, describing it, longing for it. They employ images of beautiful feet, of wolves lying down with lambs, of trees singing for joy, of swords being beaten into plowshares, of everyone sitting under their own fig tree and feasting together at the banquet of abundance with a dance in their heads.[6] All too often, however, they also have to remind God's people of *this* Kingdom, and the faithful God who reigns over it with everlasting love and justice—and of how far from and far short of God's dream they keep falling. We are not there yet. *Repent! Listen! Look!* They cry, "Listen, you that are deaf; and you that are blind, look up and see!" (Isaiah 42:18, NRSV).

The judges, prophets, and kings also remind us that we

would rather bow down to lesser kings (like our castles, institutions, nations, politics, and ideologies) even when they fail us over and over. God may be King, and all that is may be his Kingdom, but his people remain "deaf and blind" until after four hundred years of silence a voice *is* heard in the wilderness, as John the Baptist proclaims: "The time is fulfilled, and the kingdom of God has come near; repent and believe in the good news" (Mark 1:15, NRSV).

Jesus himself declares that he has come to "proclaim the good news of the kingdom of God" (Luke 4:43, NRSV). This is the core announcement that the Christ not only taught but lived and died: The Kingdom of God has come near—is here! Jesus' message and ministry both serve and are derived from, directed toward, and understood in the context of this Kingdom proclamation, and this message—that *the reign of God is at hand*—shaped his mission, and that mission now determines the mission and mantle of his followers. Jesus commissions and sends them, in all their coming and going, to "proclaim the good news, 'The kingdom of heaven has come near'" (Matthew 10:7, NRSV).[7]

The Kingdom Is Here—Say What?

So the Kingdom is here. But what *on earth* (play on words intended) does "the Kingdom of God come near" really mean?

We don't get a straight answer to this question in Scripture. Instead, Jesus describes the Kingdom with metaphors and parables. In so doing, Jesus invites us to discover the Kingdom as it is revealed in everyday life, in ordinary things, often seemingly insignificant things like shepherds and sheep, farmers and fields, bread and fish. Yet, these everyday stories and ordinary-life portrayals of the Kingdom of God confound and frustrate the experts. For instance, we read that once

> Jesus was asked by the Pharisees when the kingdom of God was coming, and he answered, "The kingdom of God is not coming with things that can be observed; nor will they say, 'Look, here it is!' or 'There it is!' For, in fact, *the kingdom of God is among you.*"
>
> LUKE 17:20-21, NRSV, EMPHASIS ADDED

And therein lies a significant clue to the nature of the Kingdom. Here and throughout the Gospels, we discover that the Kingdom of God, the reign of God breaking in and changing everything, is *Jesus* among us—*with us!* Jesus shows us the nature and intention of God's Kingdom by embodying it in all that he says and does, revealing to us what a human life truly in relationship with God, our gracious, divine King, looks like.

Jesus' presence, postures, and practices are definitely not what many expected from a king. We come to realize this most strikingly when we pay attention to how Jesus talks about the Kingdom of God. The King of God's Kingdom uses verbs that invite us into a posture entirely contrary to one of conquest, of building or advancing (emphasis added in each instance below):

- "Do not be afraid, little flock, for your Father has been pleased to *give you* the kingdom" (Luke 12:32).
- "Truly I tell you, whoever does not *receive* the kingdom of God *as a little child* will never enter it" (Luke 18:17, NRSV).
- "Come, you that are blessed by my Father, *inherit* the kingdom prepared for you from the foundation of the world" (Matthew 25:34, NRSV).
- "Listen, my beloved brothers and sisters. Has not God chosen the poor in the world to be rich in faith and to be *heirs* of the kingdom that he has promised to those who love him?" (James 2:5, NRSV).
- "In this way, entry into the eternal kingdom of our Lord and Savior Jesus Christ will be richly *provided for you*" (2 Peter 1:11, NRSV).

We are invited to receive and enter God's Kingdom. God's Kingdom come near is a gift! It is not something we can build, extend, control, or possess. The good news of the Kingdom is that God is with us and that we can receive that Kingdom, participate in it now, and inherit it in all its fullness when Jesus comes again.

The Kingdom Is Here—So What?

What, then, is *our* relationship to and role in the Kingdom? The all-encompassing picture of the heavens and earth as God's Kingdom brings a challenge, a comfort, and an invitation.

The Kingdom as Challenge

If the Kingdom of God is Jesus, the Christ, among us and in us and even now restoring relationships between God, humanity, and all creation, then some of our assumptions about God's Kingdom need to be reconsidered so that we don't end up, as Lesslie Newbigin put it, with merely an "ideology" and a "programme."[8]

We must begin by understanding that it is *God's* Kingdom, and that God in Christ is King of this Kingdom and cannot be separated from it. That might seem like a rather obvious statement, but the church has not always acted like this is so. More often than we might care to admit, we have claimed God's Kingdom on earth *as ours* to make, control, and uphold. In fact, we have often assumed that it is *our* kingdom.

For example, we have often admonished one another to *build* the Kingdom. Our strategies and mission statements have reflected this understanding and been shaped into plans, promotions, and productions to make it so. In so doing, we have declared our confidence in human reason and social progress, and in our ability to make the world a better place with our leadership techniques, management skills, fine-tuned structures, and effective systems, all of which align all too well with the politically and economically dominant in society and culture.

But God's dominion challenges the notion that the church can and ought to be extending, advancing, and/or expanding the reign of God—as if, to put it crassly, the Kingdom is our sales project, and we are its CEOs, sales reps, marketers, and distributors. The Kingdom of God, as we see it breaking in throughout the New Testament, is all about what God is doing to reveal it and to invite us to join the Spirit according to God's sovereign rule, not ours.

Moreover, our agency is disrupted over and over by the Spirit of God at work—in the world, in the other, in our neighbors. Jesus' Kingdom-in-the-flesh life turns everything upside down: the blind see, those who think they can see are declared blind, the rich are turned away empty and the poor are blessed, the lame and the lepers leap, and the dead live! Meek hearts are more important than Temple rituals; childlikeness is a necessity; women are primary witnesses. Fishermen, foreigners, tax collectors, and other sinners feast at the table *together*. Clearly, the Kingdom of God is not only at hand—it is also out of our control! And out of the control of the powers that be—whether Roman Empires, Caesars, Herods, Pilates, or righteous religious leaders.

Throughout Scripture, the Spirit and the coming of the Kingdom are found present and active, out ahead of the church in unforeseen people and unexpected places that disrupt and point beyond our agency, our preconceived notions, methodologies, and well-thought-out plans.[9] Apparently, God is quite willing and able to "build" his own Kingdom where, when, how, and with whom he chooses!

Therefore, to acknowledge, proclaim, submit to, and participate in God's Kingdom, we need a different narrative—and, one might add, a different posture from that which has pervaded centuries of particularly Euro-tribal churches. We need a narrative that asserts that God alone bears responsibility for taking care of the wheat and the weeds in the world (Matthew 13:24-30).

We need a narrative that recognizes "God's Dominion [as] a larger concept than either the church or Israel. [That] God's saving activity can happen outside either the Jewish or the Christian community. . . . [And] that activity can break into our midst quite apart from our prayers and plans."[10]

The Kingdom as Comfort

If God is sovereign over all the earth, then we do not have to fear, deny, or disengage from the world; nor do we need to conclude that everything about this world is evil and far from God. On the contrary, if the Sovereign One made, sustains, and continues to reign the world, then we can rest assured that his dominion extends over all that we are and all that we do—over science and art, work and play, leisure and culture, hearts and hands, politics and people groups, neighborhoods and nations. "O LORD, our Sovereign, how majestic is your name in all the earth!" (Psalm 8:1, NRSV).

Like the psalmists and poets before us, we can delight in God's Kingdom and in God's invitation to recognize, celebrate, and participate in it, as those made in his image who are also a part of it. This is good news! God is present and active in, as well as deeply concerned about, the world he so loves. This requires more than simply a barcode religion that guarantees our heavenly status. There is more to life than waiting to die, and there is more to this world! Heaven is closer than we think. Its hidden divine reality is right where we are, perhaps in a pillar of fire or cloud, perhaps in a rainbow, perhaps in a piece of chocolate cake or in the face of your neighbor.

God is King. God reigns, and God has a dream and a better plan than what you have been imagining and trying to construct on your own. Indeed, throughout the ages, God has communicated in a million ways "I am your power, the Kingdom and the glory," but we miss it. Somehow God's people have had trouble believing and trusting what we cannot see or prove: God's Kingship and Kingdom, God's presence and promises.

The Kingdom as Invitation

If we affirm our citizenship in God's Kingdom, then all that we are and do in our ordinary every (every!) day lives and neighborhoods should bear witness to God's Kingdom come near. By the power of the Spirit at work in us, every believer is called and equipped to embody, point to, and celebrate "God with us," for that is who we are in Christ. We are a light to the nations, the salt of the earth, blessed to be a blessing, the Kingdom of God come near (Isaiah 42:6; Acts 13:47; Matthew 5:13-14; Genesis 12:3)! Our purpose, our very being as God's people is for the sake of the reconciliation and healing of the whole world, God's Kingdom on earth. What, then, does the reign of God, manifested here and now in our midst, look like?

To address that question, we turn again to the Kingdom metaphors Jesus invites us to imagine and live into. God's Kingdom, explains Jesus, is like a mustard seed (think dandelion) planted in a field; like manure applied to a figless fig tree; like the yeast allowed to rise in a ball of dough. God's Kingdom is also like a party to which everyone is invited, where there is an abundance of food, water turned into overflowing jugs of wine, and seating that is open to all, for all are declared of equal importance, value, and consequence.

Indeed, God's Kingdom not only celebrates but brings about reconciliation (between a prodigal son and a loving father), limitless care (extended to those beaten and abandoned in ditches), connection (with the despised, outcast, and marginalized), reciprocity (fish and bread multiplied and shared, bread given even at midnight), restoration (of prostitutes, the unclean and left behind), shalom (peace and well-being) for all, and in the end, a new heaven and a new earth, where there will be no more crying, pain, or death (Revelation 21:3-5).

Following Jesus is about being who we are already called and made to be as God's people and inviting others to do the same. It's about discovering, pointing to, and participating in God's Kingdom come near right where we live in our ordinary, everyday lives. It's about embodying that Kingdom—the kindness, goodness, all-inclusive welcome, and shalom of Jesus—like Jesus, in and through Jesus, and under Jesus. He reigns!

How? By getting out of our pews and programs and

joining God at work in our neighborhoods. Why? Because in order to get beyond *our* agency, we must open ourselves to *God's* agency. And as the first followers in Acts came to realize and respond to, that happens most often outside of our Jerusalems, our synagogues, our cathedrals, our platforms, and our paradigms. Furthermore, it requires us to be attentive to and discern the Spirit at work in *those* people and places where we least expect it, where we didn't plan for it— that we might discover that *they* are actually *our* people and places, and they are God's people and places! This is the good news story: *The Kingdom comes near* in Samaritan villages where we go with nothing (Luke 10:1-12). *The Kingdom comes near* on the blocks where beggars beg; on the beach at breakfast; on hillsides when we're all hungry; in boats on stormy seas or with empty nets; beside Samaritan wells; in tax collectors' homes; among centurions, Canaanites, and Greeks; on Emmaus Roads when we are downtrodden; outside of the city; on our own; and at dinner with dirty feet, deniers, sleepyheads, liars, and betrayers.

I discover the Kingdom of God in the mustard seeds planted by my neighbors: my neighbors coming alongside a recent widow, bringing meals to a new mom, decorating a front yard with well wishes for the husband about to receive a life-saving kidney, providing childcare to the young mom with cancer. I discover the Kingdom in our community "food forest"[11] lovingly, graciously initiated by a neighborhood "Talking Gardens" group with hopes that many may benefit and that it will bear much fruit for all for decades to come. I recognize Jesus' way as neighbors gather around campfires and potlucks, sharing good food and wine, dreams and disappointments.

I point to God at work in book-club conversations about Indigenous people and our need for truth and reconciliation. I feel the welcome of God's Kingdom when new neighbors are embraced, those with developmental disabilities are included, and prejudices are dissipated at the table. I discover and participate in God's agency, first by listening, learning, reflecting and discerning *That's you God, isn't it? Your Kingdom is here*, and then by joining in, sharing gifts, sharing our lives (1 Thessalonians 2:8), and stewarding God's grace in its various forms (1 Peter 4:10) with mutual love, appreciation, humility, and respect.

These stories are signs of God's Kingdom come near in my neighborhood. There are many more, not only in my neighborhood but in yours. The sad thing is that unless we step out of our comfort zones, out of our church buildings, schedules, plans, and programs, out of our kingdoms and countries, we'll miss them. We'll miss the Kingdom of God right on our doorsteps! And we'll miss God's invitation to join in, point to, and celebrate *God's Kingdom come near!*

Maybe you didn't know it, but my hope and prayer are that you do know it now: The Kingdom of God, in flesh and blood, has moved into your neighborhood, and you have been invited to receive it, to enter into it—with all your heart, soul, mind, and strength—and to participate in it by your attentive presence and love, just like Jesus. God's Kingdom come near is also our prayer:

> *Your Kingdom come,*
> *your will be done, Lord Jesus,*
> *on earth as it is in heaven . . .*
> *for yours is the Kingdom, the power, and the glory.*

Amen.

3

A HISTORY OF KINGDOMS IN CONFLICT

Ryan Tafilowski

The year was AD 197, and things were not going well for Christians. It had been a turbulent few years in Roman political life, with each of the two previous emperors holding the position for less than three months before meeting an untimely end. Pertinax was assassinated by his own bodyguards, and his successor, Didius Julianus, was executed as part of a military coup after only sixty-six days in office. Septimius Severus was now in charge, determined to restore order. Promises of "order" always spelled doom for Christians, whom, since the days of Nero, Romans often blamed for civil unrest or natural disaster. Tertullian, a former pagan turned Christian philosopher, consoled himself with gallows humor:

"If the Tiber reaches the walls, if the Nile does not rise to the fields, if the sky doesn't move or the earth does, if there is famine, if there is plague, the cry is at once: 'The Christians to the lion!' What, all of them to one lion?"[1]

Over the course of almost two centuries, Christians had grown accustomed to playing the role of scapegoats. For Christians of Tertullian's generation, there was every reason to believe it would always be like this. But then, roughly one hundred years later, everything changed. In the fall of 312, a young general by the name of Constantine saw a cross in the clouds before a critical battle against a rival claimant to the throne. When the dust finally settled, he was the sole emperor of the Roman Empire, and he credited his victory, improbably, to the God of the Christians. By 325, Christians found themselves in the VIP section of the imperial palace, being guarded by the same soldiers who had been hunting them down just decades before. The early church historian Eusebius of Caesarea describes the scene:

> Not one of the bishops was wanting at the imperial
> banquet, the circumstances of which were splendid
> beyond description. Detachments of the body-guard
> and other troops surrounded the entrance of the
> palace with drawn swords, and through the midst of
> these the men of God proceeded without fear into
> the innermost of the imperial apartments, in which
> some were the emperor's own companions at the
> table, while others reclined on couches arranged on

either side. One might have thought that a picture
of Christ's kingdom was thus shadowed forth, and
a dream rather than reality.[2]

Eusebius couldn't believe his eyes. He had to be dreaming.
The Kingdom had come.

Or had it? "Fear God. Honor the emperor" (1 Peter 2:17,
ESV). It sounded so simple when Peter put it like that, but
what did it mean now that Christians had a share of power
and privilege? Peter's command, it seems, was difficult to follow when things were going badly, but it would prove even
more difficult when things were going well, creating unforeseen challenges. One way to tell the story of Christianity
is to tell a story of *changing fortunes*. What does it mean to
follow Jesus Christ faithfully in a world of changing political
fortunes as the social status of Christians waxes and wanes?
Christian faith has always been a precarious business.

Below, we will explore four chapters from the church's
history with the hope of learning valuable lessons about
what it means to live with Christian integrity in varying
contexts, whether we find ourselves as suspicious outsiders
in first-century Rome, energetic upstarts in ancient Ethiopia,
privileged insiders in Reformation Switzerland, or persecuted
enemies in Nazi Germany.

Suspicious Outsiders: Christians through Roman Eyes

What did Romans think about Christians? The answer is
anticlimatic: pretty much nothing. If they regarded them at

all, ordinary Romans regarded early Christians with a kind of bemused curiosity. "For almost a century Christianity went unnoticed by most men and women in the Roman Empire," writes Robert Louis Wilken. "Non-Christians [saw] the Christian community as a tiny, peculiar, antisocial, irreligious sect, drawing its adherents from the lower strata of society."[3] A Roman graffito dating to the early third century depicts a man standing at the foot of a cross on which there hangs a pathetic figure, bare bottom exposed, with the head of a jackass. The inscription reads ALEXAMENOS WORSHIPS HIS GOD. Basically, reputable Roman writers saw Christianity as a religion for losers and lunatics—fodder for graffiti artists, maybe, but not anything worth taking seriously.

The next century would show just how wrong that calculation was. By the mid-100s, Christians simply could no longer be ignored. Their communities were springing up everywhere, remarkably stubborn and resilient. Suddenly, Roman statesmen like Pliny the Younger started to see Christians as a political problem to be solved. Philosophers and intellectuals like Galen, Celsus, and Porphyry wrote long treatises aimed at discrediting Christian belief. Eventually, Christians became the object of widespread suspicion. The historian Tacitus, for example, notes in passing that Christians everywhere were "hated for their abominations" and for promoting a "deadly and dangerous superstition."[4] The most paradoxical charge levied against Christians is that they were *atheists*—and in a sense, they were.

What can we learn from our earliest brothers and sisters?

As strange as it sounds, perhaps the most important lesson is about being the right kind of "atheists." These Christians refused to bow down before the gods of Rome, who were above all gods of cruel power and violence. This "Christian atheism" took shape in all kinds of behaviors which subverted Roman religious and civic life: Christians refused to offer ritual sacrifices to the emperor; they rejected any attempt to dispose of human life, including infant exposure, abandonment, or abortion; they rejected the blood-sport spectacles, gladiatorial combat and chariot racing, which fueled the Roman economy; they rejected the abuse and degradation—sexual and economic—of women, children, slaves, and the poor, which was commonplace in Roman culture.

In the process, they transformed the moral fabric of Western civilization by "destroying the gods" of Roman paganism.[5] The names of these gods have changed, but the gods themselves haven't gone anywhere. No one today worships Mars or Venus or Ceres—but they do worship National Security, Health and Wellness, and Economic Productivity. Christians in the West increasingly find themselves cast in the same role as Roman Christians: suspicious outsiders. Can we follow the path they marked out for us? Can we unmask the gods of our age—and when we do, can we find the courage to be atheists?

Energetic Upstarts: Christian Mission in Ethiopia

When we imagine the most ancient Christian civilizations in the world, we may not immediately think of Ethiopia, but we should. When European explorers happened upon Ethiopia in the seventeenth century, they were surprised too. "No country in the world is so full of churches, monasteries, and ecclesiastics as Abyssinia [Ethiopia]," a Portuguese visitor scribbled in his travel log. "It is not possible to sing in one church without being heard by another, and perhaps by several."[6] Christian kingdoms have risen and fallen in the time since the faith first came to Africa. Syria, Egypt, Nubia— once Christian heartlands—all toppled one by one as Islam swept across east Africa from Arabia in the seventh and eighth centuries, but Ethiopia remained. Why? In part, because two shipwrecked sailors followed God into the unknown.

The Christianization of Ethiopia, in the words of Elizabeth Isichei, was the result of "a romantically unlikely chain of events."[7] The unlikely chain began with a disaster. Violent pirates waylaid a vessel bound for India as it rounded the Horn of Africa, murdering everyone on board. Well, almost everyone. Two boys were spared: Aedesius and Frumentius, a pair of Christian brothers from Tyre (modern-day Lebanon), whom the pirates pitied and sold as slaves into the royal court of King Ousanas in the capital of Aksum. Like Nehemiah, Aedesius was made cupbearer to the king, while Frumentius played the part of Joseph, whose keen intellect and practical wisdom rocketed him up the ranks of civil service. In time, Frumentius was entrusted with the king's accounts and correspondence. "From that time on," records the fourth-century historian Rufinus of Aquileia, "they were held in high honor and affection by the king."[8]

Like Daniel, Hananiah, Mishael, and Azariah before them, Aedesius and Frumentius found themselves in positions of influence at the heart of a pagan empire, where the pressure to conform to the surrounding culture was immense. Although Ousanas did not share or understand the brothers' Christian faith, he could not deny that, like the four Hebrews in Babylon, Aedesius and Frumentius were "ten times better than all the magicians and enchanters that were in all his kingdom" (Daniel 1:20, ESV). When Ousanas died, his widow begged the brothers to stay in Aksum as personal tutors to the crown prince, Ezana, "as she had no one more trustworthy in the kingdom."[9] In the end, Aedesius elected to return to Tyre, but Frumentius resolved to stay in Ethiopia.

No one could have expected what happened next. While he tutored the young prince, Frumentius leveraged his political position for the work of the gospel in Ethiopia. Through Frumentius's influence, Ezana, now king, converted to Christianity. How do we know this? Follow the money. Over time, Ezana's coins began to evolve: "His earliest inscriptions are dedicated to the South Arabian gods, Astar, Baher and Meder; later, they invoke 'The Lord of Heaven,' and, finally, the Trinity."[10]

Eventually, Frumentius was consecrated the first Bishop of Aksum by none other than Athanasius of Alexandria. In this role, he oversaw a systematic Christianization of Ethiopia by fostering networks of Christians in Aksum and coordinating the construction of churches. A century later, a contingent of missionaries known as the Nine Saints continued his work, venturing into the interior of Ethiopia, building monasteries, translating the Bible and other literature into the indigenous language of Ge'ez, and ultimately displacing paganism with a "unified and remarkably fervent Christian culture."[11]

Some Christians, particularly in the Anabaptist tradition, have been suspicious of Christians serving in political office—and not without reason. All too often, this story ends in corruption, with Christians succumbing to the corrosive temptations of power, prestige, and influence. But there are critical moments when an energetic upstart—Joseph in Egypt, Daniel in Babylon, Erastus in Rome—can alter the trajectory of an entire civilization through courageous witness to the Kingdom of God, even as they serve within the kingdoms of this world.

Although this is not the only model by which Christians can understand their relationship to political power, Frumentius's story does illustrate how effective a "top down" strategy of cultural engagement can be.[12] The story of Christianity in Ethiopia is in some ways a story about the difference that even one person can make through winsome excellence in public service and faithful stewardship of political influence. Before he became Abba Salama—"The Father of Peace"—Frumentius was a government employee. Perhaps the next Frumentius is teaching sixth grade in a public school, processing license applications at the DMV, or serving on a city council. Stranger things have happened.

From Persecuted to Persecutors: Reformation Switzerland

How had it come to this? It had all happened so fast. The trouble started when George Blaurock and Conrad Grebel, a pair of former Roman Catholic priests who had been early followers of the Swiss reformer Huldrych Zwingli, started to wonder whether the Bible really taught infant baptism. After examining the texts for himself, Blaurock didn't think so. On January 25, 1525, he asked Grebel to baptize him—or, rather, rebaptize him, since he had been baptized as an infant. It was a fateful decision, as it put this small group of dissenting Christians at odds with both Roman Catholics and other Protestants. Within a matter of months, some members of this fledgling Anabaptist ("Re-Baptizer") movement had been rounded up and imprisoned without even a hint of due process. As Blaurock recounted it later:

> Finally it reached the point that over twenty men, widows, pregnant wives, and maidens were cast miserably into dark towers, sentenced never again to see either sun or moon as long as they lived, to end their days on bread and water, and thus in the dark towers to remain together, the living and the dead, until none remained alive—there to die, to stink, and to rot.[13]

Who had locked up these Anabaptists "to die, to stink, and to rot"? It was not the Roman Catholic authorities but the Protestant magistrates of Zurich. As Reformation historian Carter Lindberg puts it, "Persecution of the Anabaptists was one point on which Protestant and Roman Catholic authorities agreed, a kind of perverse early ecumenism."[14]

This turn of events represents quite an irony. Not ten years earlier, it had been Swiss Protestants, including Zwingli, arguing that Catholic magistrates had no authority or jurisdiction to interfere with matters of religious belief, much less enforce any kind of orthodoxy. However, over the course of the 1520s, several prominent city councils, including Geneva's and Zurich's, defected from Rome and adopted the Protestant faith. Once Zwingli and others found their fortunes reversed from persecuted outsiders to privileged insiders, they began to sing a different tune. Although he had opposed government overreach into private religious convictions under other circumstances, Zwingli now urged newly converted magistrates to prosecute Anabaptists by reviving an ancient Roman law which forbade the refusal of infant baptism.

Remarkably, and at Zwingli's insistence, the city of Zurich subsequently imposed the death penalty for rebaptizers, identifying them as a threat to the civil order. In another grim irony, one of the original rebaptizers, Felix Manz, was executed by drowning on January 5, 1527. Manz wasn't the only religious dissenter to meet such a fate. In 1553, the physician and would-be theologian Michael Servetus was burned at the stake in John Calvin's Geneva for his heterodox views. While Calvin's role in the event is a matter of much debate, his critics seized the opportunity to point out a glaring hypocrisy: that "Protestant churches, once founded on the principle of scripture alone and justification by faith, had degenerated into institutions of power and vested interests that served the state."[15]

To the north in Germany, Martin Luther watched with horror as Anabaptists were murdered, burned, and drowned. It wasn't that he was sympathetic with their theology. Like Zwingli, Luther considered the Anabaptists' views on baptism to be not only erroneous but dangerous. The difference was that Luther remembered what it was like to be on the receiving end of religious persecution from the state. While the Reformation movement was still in its infancy, Luther sought to remind political authorities that

> Heresy can never be restrained by force. One will have to tackle the problem in some other way, for heresy must be opposed and dealt with otherwise than with the sword. Here God's word must do the fighting. If it does not succeed, certainly the temporal power will not succeed either, even if it were to drench the world in blood. Heresy is a spiritual matter which you cannot hack to pieces with iron, consume with fire, or drown in water.[16]

Luther saw something that can be difficult to see when we're the ones controlling the levers of power: Religious freedom cannot be granted selectively. When Zwingli argued for freedom of conscience, he meant freedom for *some* consciences.

"Remember that you were slaves in Egypt," Moses charged the people of Israel as they prepared to enter the Promised Land (Deuteronomy 15:15), with the implication that the people of God were to act with justice because they knew firsthand what injustice feels like. There is a lesson for us in this. As both Luther and Zwingli knew from personal experience, fortunes can change swiftly. Christian integrity demands that we ought not deny to other religious minorities the rights denied to us when we were in the minority.

Luther agreed with Zwingli that Anabaptists needed to be stopped, but he believed they needed to be convinced, not compelled. We want our friends and neighbors to know the fullness of the truth as made manifest in the life, death, and resurrection of Jesus Christ, and we want our nations to reflect the justice and goodness of God. But while it is tempting to try to accomplish these ends by manipulating political power, especially as Christianity seems to be declining numerically in the West, we would do well to remember Luther's words: "My friend, if you wish to drive out heresy, you must find some way to tear it first of all from the heart and completely turn men's wills away from it."[17]

God or the Devil? Christians Under Hitler

When Paul Althaus looked at his country in 1933, he saw a place he no longer recognized. By that point, he had been a Lutheran pastor and a professor of theology for over two decades, and he despaired at what he perceived to be Germany's total moral collapse: a thriving homosexual scene in Berlin, depraved films and radio programs, empty churches—Germany's Christian heritage in a state of decay. He worried about immigration. When he ventured out of his rural university town into the cities, he heard languages that weren't German being spoken by people who didn't look like Germans. He was humiliated and enraged at the German defeat during World War I, after which his nation had been guilted into accepting responsibility for the war and its catastrophic fallout.

Althaus began to doubt whether Germany had a future—until the spring of 1933. In March, Paul von Hindenburg, president of the fledgling (and flailing) Weimar Republic, appointed a young and charismatic politician as chancellor. His name was Adolf Hitler. Hitler promised to restore German glory, to protect German honor, and most importantly, to ensure that Germany remained a Christian nation. Althaus was delirious with joy at this reversal of fortunes: "Our Protestant churches have greeted the great German turning-point as a gift and miracle of God."[18]

Althaus wasn't the only one who was excited about the rise of National Socialism. When the regime signaled an early interest in incorporating Christianity into its party platform, theologians, pastors, and professors quickly got to work trying to prove their usefulness to the new administration.[19] New Testament scholars at the University of Jena, for instance, commissioned a bogus think tank, the

Institute for the Study and Eradication of Jewish Influence on German Church Life, to produce "research" showing that Jesus was not in fact Jewish but the son of a Roman soldier with Nordic bloodlines.[20] Of course, everyone knows how this story ends. Within twelve years, the Nazi war machine had systematically exterminated millions of Jews, Poles, and other "undesirables," wrought destruction across Europe and North Africa, and plunged Germany into economic, political, and spiritual ruin. In a sermon from May 1945, as allied tanks rolled into his town, Althaus finally admitted out loud what he had known to be true for some time. Germany did not just need renewal; Germany needed an *exorcism*: "The evil spirit which has possessed us these last twelve years must now be driven out."[21] Althaus and others like him thought they were opening the door to God, but they were letting in the devil.

How could they have been so wrong? There are many lessons to be learned here, but chief among them is the danger of trying to interpret political developments theologically in real time. Some German Christians were so desperate for Germany's spiritual renewal—on their own terms—that they were willing to overlook the obvious chauvinism, brutality, and wickedness of the National Socialist party well into the 1930s. One of the great tragedies of this chapter of the church's history is that Christian support for National Socialism dramatically changed the trajectory of Germany's history, doing irreversible damage to the witness of the church. Even now, over seventy years later, Europe is still experiencing the consequences.

But not everybody followed in the apostasy. Paradoxically, some Christians in Germany were enthusiastic supporters of the Nazi government while others were its persecuted enemies. There were dissenting voices, a coalition of German Protestants who resisted Nazi interference with religious affairs. This group came to be known as the Confessing Church.

The Confessing Church demonstrated incredible courage in many ways, but perhaps its most enduring legacy is the Barmen Declaration, a statement of faith written in defiance of Nazi ideology. The singular achievement of the declaration, it seems to me, is its unwavering commitment to the supremacy of Jesus Christ, over and above any political figure or philosophy: "Jesus Christ, as he is attested for us in the Holy Scripture, is the one Word of God which we have to hear and which we have to trust and obey in life and in death." Therefore, the statement continues, "We reject the false doctrine [that] the Church is permitted to abandon the form of its message and order according to its own pleasure or to changes in prevailing ideological and political convictions."[22] When we elevate one politician or another as the embodiment of God's will for our nation, we violate the lordship of Christ, which should be the standard by which we make any political decision. There is only one Word of God whom we are to trust and obey: Jesus Christ, "ruler of the kings of the earth" (Revelation 1:5).

Integrity through Changing Fortunes

Historically, Christians have a mixed record of faithfulness and failure when it comes to engaging with political power. Each chapter of the church's story is a chapter in our story too. What can we learn from our brothers and sisters who have gone before us? The earliest Christians model for us the kind of courage it takes to live distinctively in the midst of a suspicious and sometimes hostile culture. Frumentius teaches us the value of Christian excellence in civil service. In the age of the Reformation, we can see both the allure and the pitfalls of wielding political influence against outsiders. The struggle for the soul of the German church under Hitler highlights how disastrous it can be when Christians pledge their allegiance to an earthly power instead of to Jesus Christ.

If there is any one lesson to draw from our historical survey, perhaps it is this: Christians are called to *integrity* through changing fortunes. Our principles and values—the refusal of idolatry, love of our (non-Christian) neighbors, and commitment to the lordship of Christ—should remain the same no matter our relationship to earthly kingdoms: whether suspicious outsider, privileged insider, persecuted enemy, or anything in between.

You and I are not suffering under Septimius Severus. We are not shipwrecked off the Horn of Africa. We are not wrangling with magistrates in Zurich. We are not struggling for the faith in the shadow of Hitler. But make no mistake: Sooner or later, our fortunes will change, for good or for ill.

Will we walk with integrity when they do?

4

UNDER THE AUTHORITY
OF ANOTHER

Derek Vreeland

THE FIRST NATION UNDER GOD was the people of Israel.

In choosing and establishing a covenant with Abram, the God of creation chose to bring God's benevolent rule to the earth through the people of God. The gathering of God's people wouldn't be tangential to God's saving activity; rather, this gathering of called-out ones would be integral to God's work of redemption and restoration. In fact, the bulk of the Bible could be read as the story of the people of God learning to walk in the ways of God for the sake of the justice of God on the earth. Their steps, and at times missteps, were almost always taken while they were living under pagan authority (excluding the time of the monarchy when Israel—and later Judah, after Solomon's kingdom divided—had their own kings). These pagan rulers included the Egyptian pharaoh, the Assyrian and Babylonian kings, and the Persian rulers, and by the time of Jesus and the apostles, the people of God were under the boot of the Roman Caesars.

One thing remained consistent for the people of God when they found themselves governed by other nations or empires: They believed their God was king. The prayer and worship of Israel was filled with this royal proclamation, particularly in the Psalms:

- "The LORD is king forever and ever" (Psalm 10:16, NRSV).
- "Lift up your heads, O gates! and be lifted up, O ancient doors! that the King of glory may come in. Who is this King of glory? The LORD of hosts, he is the King of glory" (Psalm 24:9-10, NRSV).
- "The LORD sits enthroned over the flood; the LORD sits enthroned as king forever" (Psalm 29:10, NRSV).
- "The LORD is king, he is robed in majesty . . . your throne is established from of old; you are from everlasting" (Psalm 93:1-2, NRSV).
- "The LORD is king! Let the earth rejoice; let the many coastlands be glad!" (Psalm 97:1, NRSV).
- "For the LORD is a great God, and a great King above all gods" (Psalm 95:3, NRSV).
- "The LORD is king; let the peoples tremble! He sits enthroned upon the cherubim; let the earth quake!" (Psalm 99:1, NRSV).

The God of Abraham, Isaac, and Jacob didn't look like the gods of the other tribes and empires surrounding ancient Israel. This God was not merely the king of one Semitic tribe called "the Hebrews." The ancient people of God had the audacity to declare in their prayers that their God was king of the nations. Again we turn our attention to the Psalms:[1]

- "For the LORD, the Most High, is awesome, a great king *over all the earth.* . . . For God is the king of *all the earth*; sing praises with a psalm. God is king *over the nations*; God sits on his holy throne" (Psalm 47:2, 7-8, NRSV).
- "Say among the nations, 'The LORD is king! The world is firmly established; it shall never be moved. He will judge *the peoples* with equity'" (Psalm 96:10, NRSV).
- "The LORD has established his throne in the heavens, and his kingdom rules *over all*" (Psalm 103:19, NRSV).

Their belief in God as King over the earth didn't imply God was merely King over spiritual matters, in what we modern people would call "religion." Their faith in God implied God was King over the entirety of their lives, their families, and their civic life together and with their neighbors. Such commitment and loyalty to a God who ruled over all nations, tribes, and tongues would certainly create tension among the people of God from the very beginning when they found themselves enslaved in Egypt. The tension re-emerged after Israel and Judah fell to foreign invaders and the people of God found themselves in exile in Babylon, where they wrestled anew with their identity as the children of Abraham living in a strange land. The tension didn't resolve when they were under Persian rule, and it certainly intensified when Jesus and the apostles proclaimed the gospel of the Kingdom of God throughout the Jewish and pagan world ruled by Caesar.

This tension between their fidelity to God as King and the necessity of living as a subjugated people under the rule of earthly kings manifested in questions of trust and allegiance. With whom would the people of God ultimately align themselves? Whom would they put their confidence in for their own well-being? Which ruler would they ultimately trust for their sense of corporate identity? Again we turn to the Psalms for answers embedded in Israel's worship and prayer: "It is better to rely on the LORD than to put any trust in flesh. It is better to rely on the Lord than to put any trust in rulers" (Psalm 118:8-9).[2] The princes and rulers, noblemen and pagan kings could not, in the end, be trusted for the well-being of the people of God. The God of creation, the one who entered a covenant with Abraham, was the one reigning King in whom the people of God could trust.

A Suffering Community under the Egyptian Pharaoh

Trusting the God of Israel as King would prove difficult when the ancient people of God found themselves enslaved in Egypt. Famine brought Jacob and his sons to Egypt, where Joseph, the beloved son of Jacob, had risen in position and authority. The pharaoh who had elevated Joseph welcomed Jacob's family to experience "the best of the land of Egypt" (Genesis 45:18, NRSV). Jacob's family, the Israelites, flourished in Egypt and began to grow in number. When another pharaoh (who didn't have history with Joseph) came into power, he feared the Israelites and enslaved them, oppressing them with harsh labor. They were tasked with making bricks, and they complied. Even though the Israelites obeyed their taskmasters, the Egyptians grew to hate them. Violence followed racial hate as Pharaoh commanded that all Israelite boys be thrown into the Nile River at birth. Two Hebrew midwives refused to obey the command to commit infanticide because they feared God (Exodus 1:17). Their allegiance to the life-affirming ways of God prompted an act of civil disobedience which resulted in the blessing of God, even as the people of God continued to experience harsh demands from those who hated them. God's people suffered, but their suffering didn't go unnoticed. God heard the cries that reverberated from the earth, and he raised up a deliverer to confront the pharaoh and lead the people of God out of suffering, out of Egypt.

Moses, who was unsure of his abilities, emerged as an unlikely deliverer. He told God of his lack of eloquence and his struggle with public speaking, but God reassured him that as he stood before Pharaoh, God would be with him and give him the words to say. Moses and his brother, Aaron, went to Pharaoh and asked him to let the people of God go. Pharaoh refused. He wasn't about to let his cheap labor force go free, so he instructed the taskmasters to continue to demand the same quota of bricks without supplying the Israelites with straw. Therefore the taskmasters forced the people of God to collect their own straw to produce bricks. Even though they had suffered so much, the people of God complied. When receiving the new demands, "the people scattered throughout the land of Egypt, to gather stubble for straw" (Exodus 5:12, NRSV).

The Israelites submitted to the unjust demands of the Egyptian taskmasters and were beaten when their quota was not met. Their suffering only increased as they obeyed. The cruel regulations and violence could be seen on their backs, and the despair could be heard in their groaning. Their suffering would not be indefinite because God heard them, and through Moses, God would soon liberate them. The God of Israel, who is free from the constraints of coercion and violence, made humanity in the very image of that freedom. The slavery and harsh labor experienced by God's people was the opposite of freedom. Moses spoke to Pharaoh again. Pharaoh remained stubborn, so plagues came. The Righteous One swept through Egypt. Moses led the people out of Egypt, and God performed a miracle: He led his people through the waters of the Red Sea. Their liberation was complete, and the freed people sang a celebratory song of liberation in praise of their God:

I will sing to the Lord, for he has triumphed
    gloriously. . . .
The Lord is a warrior;
    the Lord is his name. . . .
In the greatness of your majesty you overthrew your
    adversaries. . . .
Who is like you, O Lord, among the gods?
    Who is like you, majestic in holiness,
    awesome in splendor, doing wonders?

EXODUS 15:1, 3, 7, 11, NRSV

They closed their song renewing their allegiance to God as King with the words "The Lord will reign forever and ever" (Exodus 15:18, NRSV). According to pastor and professor John Goldingay, God's intervention in Pharaoh's domination of the Israelites caused God to enter "a new sphere of activity. The God of the clan becomes the God of history and the God of politics, battling with Egyptian pharaoh and defeating him."[3] The people of God endured suffering as they obeyed their earthly rulers, but their suffering was limited. God as King made a political move and liberated the people who remained loyal to the covenant and to the God of Abraham, Isaac, and Jacob.

A Subversive Community under the Babylonian Kings

The people of God would wander in the wilderness for decades before Joshua, Moses' aide, led them into the Promised Land. There they flourished in a land flowing with milk and honey, and even though God remained their King, they became jealous of other nations and tribes and demanded a king of their own. God accommodated them with an earthly king. The effectiveness of this monarchy was inevitably short-lived, as the kingdom built by David fractured into two. Various kings came and went from this divided kingdom until the northern kingdom was conquered by the Assyrians and the southern kingdom fell to the Babylonians.

The Babylonian king destroyed the Temple and rounded up the people of God, deporting them to Babylon. They watched as their city was ravaged, their loved ones were killed, and their holy Temple was destroyed. When they reached Babylon, they leaned deeply into lament: "By the rivers of Babylon—there we sat down and there we wept when we remembered Zion. On the willows there we hung up our harps" (Psalm 137:1-2, NRSV). In Babylon the people of God, displaced from their homeland, would learn to thrive in their distinctiveness as the children of Abraham shaped by the Torah and their traditions (yet without their Temple). To do so they practiced what Old Testament scholar Walter Brueggemann calls a "local tradition" to resist the totalizing and dominating presence of the Babylonian Empire. For Brueggemann, "'local tradition' looks at the world differently than the empire; it tells an alternative and opposing story to that of empire."[4] Their sacred story and the sacred law of Moses would keep them from enculturating into the dominating ways and means of empire. But resisting the values of Babylon would not be easy.

Early on in the Exile, the people of God found themselves with little options, much like when they were enslaved in Egypt, so they submitted to the governing officials. In fact, for a time, submission to Babylon was in keeping with submission to God. Through Jeremiah, God calls King Nebuchadnezzar of Babylon "my servant" (Jeremiah 25:9, 27:6, 43:10). Brueggemann calls this cooperation and submission to Babylon both short-lived and a matter of pragmatism: "In the end, however, the local tradition of Israel cannot collude with empire precisely because YHWH, the God of the local tradition, is also the God of international politics who will not continue to collude with Babylon."[5] God used Babylon instrumentally as a punishment for Israel's idolatry and injustice, but the purpose of this punishment was to bring his people back into covenant fidelity with the God who brought them out of Egypt.

God's goal in punishment wasn't merely punitive but was also restorative. God never intended exile to be the permanent legacy of God's covenant people. His ultimate purpose was and is the coming of the Kingdom of God and new creation, as revealed in the coming of Jesus. Yet the people of God in Babylon experienced exile as a present reality. So while enduring the punishment of exile, they learned to live under Babylonian authority but always with the hope that a "righteous Branch," a king in the royal lineage of David, would come and rescue God's people (Jeremiah 33:15, NRSV). This hope empowered them to live in a way that was both submissive and subversive while they made temporary homes in Babylon. They submitted to the imperial authorities and "[sought] the welfare of the city" (Jeremiah 29:7, NRSV)—all as they stood in the light of God's truth.

Daniel and his friends quite literally took a stand. Daniel, Shadrach, Meshach, and Abednego had risen in predominance in Babylon. King Nebuchadnezzar even promoted Daniel to a position of authority in the king's court. Then came the golden statue and the imperial edict to worship the image when prompted. Daniel and his friends had been formed in the Jewish local tradition of fidelity to the one God of creation, and they would worship no idols, even under the threat of execution. When examined by Nebuchadnezzar, Daniel's friends were clear about this: "Be it known to you, O king, that we will not serve your gods and we will not worship the golden statute that you have set up" (Daniel 3:18, NRSV). They were ordered to be executed by fire but were miraculously rescued. Similarly, Daniel continued to worship the true God when threatened with death by lions, and God saved the life of his faithful servant.

Daniel and his friends had climbed the social ranks within the empire, but they had been shaped by a tradition that oriented their lives around worshiping the one true living God. This formation would limit their submission to the imperial authorities. Their life of prayer and devotion to the Torah fueled their subversion. Therefore, when King Darius established an ordinance prohibiting prayer directed toward anyone but the king, Daniel continued to kneel toward Jerusalem and pray three times a day. The authorities caught Daniel violating the king's orders while he was "praying and seeking mercy before his God" (Daniel 6:11, NRSV). Not even a den of lions could deter Daniel from the practices of the local tradition he had learned. The propaganda of the empire couldn't defeat the conviction held deeply in the hearts of God's people that God reigned as King. They made some necessary concessions toward civic rulers, but as Brueggemann notes: "Behind that pragmatism, however, is a durable theological conviction that regards the empire as secondary and therefore not to be excessively respected or embraced."[6]

A Spirit-Empowered Community under the Roman Caesars

From the rootedness of a people who were known as both a suffering and a subversive community living under the authority of pagan rulers, Jesus has been building his church. When Jesus asked his disciples who people were saying he was, they responded that people thought he was one of the prophets. When Jesus asked the disciples who *they* thought he was, Peter made a bold declaration: "You are the Messiah, the Son of the living God" (Matthew 16:16, NRSV). Peter's confession would become part of the bedrock of the church. Peter and all subsequent believers believed Jesus was the long-awaited Messiah, the true King of Israel. He was the promised King whose "authority shall grow continually, and there shall be endless peace for the throne of David and his kingdom. He will establish and uphold it with justice and with righteousness from this time onward and forevermore" (Isaiah 9:7, NRSV).

Jesus came not only as a Jewish king in the royal lineage of David. Jesus also came in the power of the Spirit as the *Word made flesh*, the full embodiment of Israel's God. The ancient people of God believed he reigned as the one true King over all nations and empires—including the Roman Empire, in which Jesus and the apostles announced the good news of God's Kingdom. Early followers of Jesus believed him to be Lord, which meant, in all sorts of ways, that Caesar was not.[7] This reshuffling of political authority meant that the followers of Jesus would need a new reliance upon the Spirit of God to determine how they would exist as loyal servants of the Kingdom of God living in the shadow of the empire.

The Romans governed with sweeping and unparalleled might. They had been ruling over Judea for a little over a generation before the birth of Jesus with what N. T. Wright and Michael Bird call "an insensitive arrogance that constantly bordered on provocation to rebellion."[8] They brought a peace project to the Mediterranean world, the *Pax Romana*, through undeterred military power. The people loyal to the God of Israel were forced to accept Roman rule or suffer the possibility of extinction. Those in Judea who aligned themselves with Rome, like Herod the Great, were rewarded. The Roman Senate bestowed on Herod the title "King of the Jews." Those who failed to pledge their allegiance to Rome and fought against the purposes of the empire were violently suppressed by crucifixion. Well before Jesus came announcing the Kingdom of God, would-be Jewish kings had sprung up from Galilee leading rebellions against Rome. Each time they were met with brutal defeat. The Roman general Varus ended one such rebellion by crucifying some two thousand Jewish revolutionaries.[9] The Roman governors expected unequivocal obedience to Roman law because submission to the empire was the way to peace—Roman peace.

Jesus came preaching the gospel of the Kingdom of God, promising it would lead to a different kind of peace. He told his disciples, "Peace I leave with you; my peace I give to you. I do not give to you as the world gives. Do not let your hearts be troubled, and do not let them be afraid" (John 14:27, NRSV). In the face of Roman brutality, Jesus told his followers to reject fear and accept the peace he was giving, a peace that would be made known by the Holy Spirit. Jesus had announced his departure but promised to send the Holy Spirit to be with them as a helper and guide. The renewed people of God—comprised of both Jews and Gentiles, slaves and free people, men and women, young and old, rich and poor—would be a Spirit-empowered community marked by love, joy, and peace. God the Holy Spirit would enable them to confess that Jesus is indeed Lord. Paul wrote, "No one can say 'Jesus is Lord' except by the Holy Spirit" (1 Corinthians 12:3, NRSV). The Spirit would come to shape them into the image of Jesus and empower them to be witnesses to the life, miracles, teaching, death, resurrection, and ascension of Jesus, reminding them of everything Jesus had taught them (including giving to Caesar what was his).

Jesus didn't specifically teach his followers how to live as the people under the authority of another, but in trying to trap him, the Pharisees once asked him about paying taxes. Jesus famously responded, "Give to Caesar what belongs to Caesar, and give to God what belongs to God" (Matthew 22:21, NLT). In typical Jesus fashion, this answer swirled around the hearts and minds of the Pharisees, but it didn't spring their trap. Within this masterful response Jesus shows the complexities involved in living as citizens of the Kingdom of God and living as citizens in the empires of men. The early communities formed by the apostles around the life, death, and resurrection of Jesus would find that in the end Caesar, as a representation of civic authority, would get something. Caesar would get their tax money. Caesar would be included in their prayers (1 Timothy 2:1-2). Caesar would get their respect (1 Peter 2:17). Caesar would get their compliance (Titus 3:1-2). But Caesar wouldn't get everything because the one true God of creation was the ultimate King. Caesar wouldn't get their complete allegiance because their faith was in King Jesus. Those who received the gospel extended fidelity, allegiance, and loyalty to King Jesus over and above all other kings and earthly rulers. Caesar may have received coins from the hands of Jesus' followers, but he didn't receive devotion from their hearts.

The early Christians were not outright rebels, flippantly casting aside the laws of the land. Those Christians in Rome knew the words of Paul's admonishment well: "Let every person be subject to the governing authorities; for there is no authority except from God, and those authorities that exist have been instituted by God" (Romans 13:1, NRSV). Paul's directive wasn't one of uncritical obedience but of submission to earthly authorities insofar as they align themselves with the authority of God, from whom they derive their authority.[10]

The followers of Jesus recognized the role of civic government to provide social order for the flourishing of cities, yet they imbibed the spirit of the ancient people of God living as exiles and lived as a subversive people. They showed a sign of honor to Caesar by submitting themselves to Roman authority. Yet like Peter before the high priest and elders of Israel, these early Christians were steadfast in their allegiance to the God revealed in Jesus. "We must obey God rather than any human authority" (Acts 5:29, NRSV) remained their primary way of living as dual citizens. In fact, they would disobey an unjust law and accept the suffering which would follow in acts of disobedience because, in the words of Martin Luther King Jr., "an unjust law is no law at all."[11] God the Holy Spirit would lead them to discern which laws were unjust.

The Spirit-led community of Jesus followers bore the twin characteristics of the ancient people of God in that they were willing to persist as a *suffering* community particularly because they were a *subversive* community. Pledging their allegiance to King Jesus would put them at odds with the empire time and time again. The empire required total devotion, total loyalty to the Roman way of life, and gave little room for people to share their loyalties to another ruler. The people who professed "Jesus is Lord" swore loyalty to Jesus as King over all kings and Lord over all lords. The resurrected and ascended Jesus had received all power and authority from God the Father. All earthly rulers derived their authority from him. So if the followers of Jesus discerned by the Spirit that the edicts given by Caesar were not rooted in the justice of God or the ways of Jesus, they faced no dilemma in what they would do. They would respect Caesar but they would obey God, trusting the power and presence of God the Holy Spirit to sustain them in their acts of subversion and comfort them when suffering came.

We belong to that same community. We worship the same Lord Jesus and imbibe the same Holy Spirit. Who we are as the *modern* people of God in the twenty-first century is rooted in the *ancient* people of God suffering the indignity of slavery to the Egyptians. Today we live in a world without the harshness of racial slavery, but as followers of Jesus we accept the suffering that comes when we are misunderstood, maligned, and even hated because of our identity as Kingdom citizens squarely aligned with the values of King Jesus.

When the civic authorities in the country where we live shape our culture in a way that challenges the rhythms of the Kingdom of God, we choose a subversive path like the people of God living as exiles in Babylon. We turn down the imperial noise coming from both Fox News and MSNBC and turn up our "local tradition" rooted in prayer, Scripture, worship, and other practices that draw our attention to the presence of God with us. Through these practices we experience the stabilizing effect of God the Holy Spirit keeping us grounded in the ways of love, empowering us to become more and more like the Jesus to whom we pledge our full and undivided allegiance.

5

THE ETHICS
OF ALLEGIANCE

Sean Palmer

ASIA WAS THE STRANGEST GIRL IN SIXTH GRADE. She didn't talk much. Not many of us talked to her. She wore an African head scarf. Every day. In Stone Mountain, Georgia, in 1986, that was a bit much for a bunch of southern kids who had never met many people unlike themselves. But Asia wasn't *that* unlike me. She was African American, like me, one of the few of us in our predominantly White school and class.

Stone Mountain, you might remember, was name-checked in Martin Luther King Jr.'s "I Have a Dream" speech—and for good reason. During the Civil War the mountain was used as an armory by southern traitors to the US government. During Reconstruction, Stone Mountain

71

served as a rallying point for the Ku Klux Klan. Even today, the side of Stone Mountain is the home of an etching of Stonewall Jackson, Robert E. Lee, and Jefferson Davis, men who rebelled against the Union in order to uphold human, chattel slavery. They are celebrated for pursuing the continuation of slavery.

Stone Mountain is where Asia and I grew up.

We should have been allies.

We should have been friends.

We weren't!

We weren't friends because Asia was a bridge too far, even for the other Black kids. She was *African* African American. She wore traditional African garb, like I said, a head scarf. Her lunch was packed not with Black, southern food but with *African* food. But what made Asia truly different, even distinct from the other Black students, was that she was a Jehovah's Witness. Even more strange, each morning, during the daily school announcements and before class began, when the rest of the class stood to recite the Pledge of Allegiance, Asia didn't.

She sat!

She was the only one who sat.

She sat. And she didn't recite the pledge.

As a sixth grader, I thought that was odd. *America is* our *country*, I thought. *Love it. Accept it. Respect it.* That meant standing for the pledge. I also wondered what the big deal was. The pledge was perfunctory, an empty signifier that launched our school day and didn't mean all that much. I did not see an obvious disconnect. Either the pledge meant something and she should join us in reciting it—or it was empty, meant nothing, and I shouldn't care if she, or anyone, ever recited it.

Turns out, Asia thought more deeply about the Pledge of Allegiance than I ever had. She knew what I didn't. She knew allegiance ought to mean something. And the Pledge is just the tip of the iceberg.

The Meaning of Allegiance

As I got older and I met other Christians from around the globe, both within and outside my denomination, I discovered it wasn't only people like Asia but folks much closer to me who held the same beliefs I did theologically but who also opted out of offering allegiance through the Pledge. One was a university English professor, a theologically and politically conservative woman with a quote from Shakespeare always at the ready. When I asked her when she began opting out of reciting the Pledge, she responded, "The moment I understood what *allegiance* meant." Her response stunned me. She wasn't protesting anything. Her silence wasn't centered on her feelings about America or history or even contemporary Left/Right politics. She wasn't making a statement about the state, she was making a statement about her life being aligned with her words. And words mean something. Opting out was not about saying or not saying the Pledge of Allegiance as a function of her citizenship in America (as most people project when others don't participate in America's national liturgies).[1] It was about her relationship with God, her allegiance.

What does it mean to give our allegiance to something or someone? Matthew W. Bates gives us some much-needed clarity regarding the word *allegiance* in Christian perspective in his book *Salvation by Allegiance Alone*:

> With regard to eternal salvation, rather than speaking of belief, trust, or faith in Jesus, we should speak instead of fidelity to Jesus as cosmic Lord or allegiance to Jesus the king. This, of course, is not to say that the best way to translate every occurrence of *pistis* (and related terms) is always or even usually "allegiance." Rather it is to say that allegiance is the best macro-term available to us that can describe what God requires from us for eternal salvation. It is the best term because it avoids unhelpful English-language associations that have become attached to "faith" and "belief," as well as limitations in the "trust" idea, and at the same time it captures what is most vital for salvation—mental assent, sworn fidelity, and embodied loyalty.[2]

Fidelity and *allegiance* shock our religious sensibilities. They jolt our spiritual expectations. Christians have relegated "faith," "belief," and even "trust" to a spiritual, Sunday-morning realm. When faith is understood as allegiance (loyalty to a government or sovereign), or as Bates says, "mental assent, sworn fidelity, and embodied loyalty" rather than "belief" (a set of tenants we can easily forget we hold, like believing in the reality of gravity), we are invited into a more robust engagement about the competing loyalties grasping for our attention and affections. Now we come face-to-face with the reality that allegiance asks a particular ordering of our inward being and our outer actions and priorities—our "embodied loyalty."

This understanding forces unavoidable conflicts and questions. If allegiance to the state means anything, must it mean the same thing that allegiance to God means? Can I offer my allegiance to God if I have already offered it to the state? And what does this understanding of allegiance mean for the other competing sovereigns of life? My company or career? My spouse? My children? My political party? How can I possibly serve God and render my fidelity to the state simultaneously? What should I think of the state and friends, family, political leaders, and other powers who suggest I should give allegiance to the state or risk their sanction, punishment, or exclusion?

Some would argue this is all simply a matter of priorities. But again, this tactic disregards or ignores what words *actually* mean, and whether words even mean anything at all. One cannot have "priorities." One can only have an ordered agenda. One item, by definition, must come *prior* to others. If we are not honest about the reality of what we are saying— or told to say—we have backed our way into a cynical corner where we must confess that our words (which find their origin in our hearts) don't mean anything. If our words don't mean anything, they should not be trusted. And if we know we are saying words that don't mean anything, *we* should not be trusted. When it comes to our allegiance (both the words we speak and the murkier allegiance which lingers in our hearts), followers of Jesus must be clearer regarding our intentions. The Kingdom of God means God's total reign, and that must mean something in the grit and dirt of our lived experience. Citizens who hold the state and God as equally worthy of allegiance might just be trying too hard to make oil and water mix.

The Salvific, Incompetent State

The New Testament appears to give us straightforward and crisp direction. In his seminal sermon, the Lord teaches, "No one can serve two masters; for a slave will either hate the one and love the other, or be devoted to the one and despise the other. You cannot serve God and wealth" (Matthew 6:24, NRSV). If you think money and the state are not the same, consider that one of the chief functions of the state is to regulate the economy, tax the citizenry, disperse funds, and so on. In America, for instance, the primary function of the United States Congress is fiduciary. They control the checkbook. When the FBI couldn't punish Al Capone for murder, the Treasury Department got him on tax evasion. The state primarily exists to regulate the economy. This is what politicians mean when they argue policy is enacted or not enacted because of "American interests." Jesus says you cannot serve two masters.

Jesus also speaks of a rightly oriented relationship with God in totalizing language:

> When the Pharisees heard that he had silenced the
> Sadducees, they gathered together, and one of them,
> a lawyer, asked him a question to test him. "Teacher,
> which commandment in the law is the greatest?"
> He said to him, "'You shall love the Lord your God
> with *all* your heart, and with *all* your soul, and
> with *all* your mind.' This is the greatest and first
> commandment."
>
> MATTHEW 22:34-38, NRSV, EMPHASIS ADDED

Jesus, it seems, is not a fan of wiggle room. On its face, who can hear these words from Jesus and hold allegiance in any degree, spoken or unspoken, to any other government or sovereign besides Jesus? After all, *all* means *all*!

Yet if the teachings of the Lord are so clear, how come so many American Christians readily, without hesitation, and some believing it honors God, pledge their allegiance to a flag and the republic for which it stands, by which we mean the state? As we've seen, the issue is more layered than just the words we say. On offer is not just an allegiance in word but an allegiance of the heart to the state. Jesus so clearly states that no one can serve two masters, but we keep trying. Are we stupid, deceived, or something else?

Plus, when asked, no orthodox Christian would affirm the state as being in possession of salvific power. In fact, many would argue that the state cannot even coherently conceive a fair and equitable tax code; properly regulate immigration; constructively raise and educate children; make right and just decisions regarding war; manifest a fair, unbiased, and impartial justice system; or manage to manage much of anything they should manage. Still, we offer our allegiance to a state many—on the political Left *and* Right—would argue is competent. What sense does that make?

In fact, offering allegiance to the state, with all her incompetencies and tensions, does not make intellectual sense, but it does have a moral emotional ethic.[3] Why? Because we love our country. My father spent his early educational career as an American history teacher. He passed on to me a love of history, and of American history in particular. I love and enjoy the stories of Alexander Hamilton, Dred Scott, Harriet Tubman, Abraham Lincoln, FDR, world wars, and all the rest. I marvel at the bravery and scientific accomplishment it took to land a human on the moon and the moral and civil courage of examples and leaders like Ruby Bridges, Rosa Parks, and Fred Gray. I feasted on these stories as a child and still do as an armchair historian.

Not only are these tales interesting and inspiring, they are also formative. I cannot completely understand myself and my place in the world apart from the American story. Like any healthy human, I love me! That means I love the story which created me. I love my country. When most people award the state allegiance, what we might well mean is *I love this place. I love this story. I love that I'm part of its story.* Moral emotion—love, shame, guilt, pride, gratitude, etc.—ethics plays an enormous part in how we discern what is right and what is wrong. Our confusion around allegiance is a product of these moral emotion ethics, particularly love and gratitude and shame and guilt.

Don't believe me? Choose to not participate in America's national liturgies and chronicle how long it takes before someone asks whether you "love your country." How long will it take before you're asked if you're ungrateful or a part of the "blame (read: shame) America first" crowd?

Love It or Leave It?

Our moral emotion ethics are the problem! We love so much that we have fallen for the lie that all love is right and good love—or, at least, that love will never force our allegiances into competition. But as Augustine has directed us, our loves can be disordered.[4] The trouble is that contemporary Christians are so committed to love of state that we rarely question if that love has become disordered.

When NFL player Colin Kaepernick refused to stand for the national anthem—a step he took after it was suggested to him by Army veteran and NFL long snapper Nate Boyer— he was reviled as someone who hated his country. Super Bowl–winning coach Mike Ditka said if he felt that way, he should leave. Going even farther, after Nike produced an ad featuring Kaepernick, Reverend Mack Morris, the senior pastor at Woodridge Baptist Church in Mobile, Alabama, took to the pulpit to destroy his personal Nike apparel. There was no discussion of ordered loves and where patriotism fits in the ranking of allegiances. What was most striking about Reverend Morris's message that Sunday was not the destruction of his personal property but his reasoning: "Some of our values are being strained . . ."

Which values?

And what is "being strained" by Morris, sitting at home after worship on a Sunday afternoon watching the NFL or a Nike ad during the Super Bowl? Reverend Morris was not alone in his indignation. Across the country there were #BurnNike protests. Angered Americans gathered to burn their own property because Nike created an advertisement with a second-string quarterback who opted out of the national liturgy.

What I want us to see here is that for too many, love of country has become fabulously disordered. Many have not thought to order their loves at all. To love your country means to give it allegiance and demonize those who question whether that allegiance is misplaced (as doubtless some of you are doing right now). To question love and allegiance to the state brings more than suspicion on those who ask the questions; it brings contempt. For many, Kaepernick failed to appropriately love his country. In turn, they would display their love of country through their vehemence about his lack of love. What his critics missed is that Colin Kaepernick, too, is a Christian and his protest was fueled by his belief that American policing demonstrated a lack of love for Black and Brown people. It was his commitment to neighbor love which fueled his protest. When asked his reasoning, Kaepernick replied, "I am not going to stand up to show pride in a flag for a country that oppresses black people and people of color. To me, this is bigger than football and it would be selfish on my part to look the other way. There are bodies in the street and people getting paid leave and getting away with murder."[5] His protest was not a holdout for a new contract, like a myriad of athletes have done, but for "black people and people of color." It was about not being "selfish." We can agree or disagree about the nature of Kaepernick's protest, but what inflamed people like Reverend Morris is Kaepernick's refusal of reflexive allegiance and the ordering of loves.

The Endless Immensity

So, where does that leave the American Christian community? Knowing these tensions exist, what are we supposed to do? How do we render to God what is God's and to Caesar what is Caesar's? The only way forward is to give Christians a bigger, better, and more beautiful vision than their country; a vision that dwarfs national allegiance and reveals those who seek it to be as petty as children fighting over the larger portion of a split peanut-butter-and-jelly sandwich when an endless buffet is on offer. As Antoine de Saint-Exupéry writes: "If you want to build a ship, don't drum up people to collect wood and don't assign them tasks and work, but rather teach them to long for the endless immensity of the sea."[6] Have Christians become befuddled by misguided loves because our anemic love of God has made the state seem like an equally accessible and equally powerful alternative? A nation's endgame, however, is to make the nation great. The church's endgame is to announce and enact the Kingdom of God. And the only way to partner with God in the renewing of the world is to do for the world what Jesus has done for the world: Love it.

Our problem is not that we love our country too much, it's that we love our neighbors too little. In Jesus' economy our neighbor, not our nation, is the *telos* of our love: "'Love the Lord your God with all your heart, and with all your soul, and with all your mind, and with all your strength.' . . . 'You shall love your neighbor as yourself.' There is no commandment greater than these" (Mark 12:30-31, NRSV). Barbara Brown Taylor puts it this way, "The only clear line I draw these days is this: when my religion tries to come between me and my neighbor, I will choose my neighbor. . . . Jesus never commanded me to love my religion."[7]

She's right.

Jesus never commanded his followers to love the state. We can only give to Caesar until doing so interferes with Jesus' command to love our neighbors, for in loving our neighbors, we fulfill the Lord's command to love him with our "all." Furthermore, we must keep in mind that when Jesus is asked the world-narrowing question "Who is my neighbor?" he responded with the parable of the Good Samaritan, a story which compels love and pushes it across religious, national, and cultural boundaries. Jesus teaches us that when we think of our "neighbor," we should think of the entire world, particularly those who are vulnerable, abandoned, and abused. If our concept of neighbor is our friend down the street, we are thinking far too small. The ethical question when it comes to the ethics of allegiance is this: Does offering my allegiance to this fulfill the Shema?[8]

Allegiance to the state must always be contingent on the state's current position as it blesses or burdens my neighbor. And because the state is multifaceted, always performing some good and some evil, it is unworthy of a Christian's unquestioning and reflexive allegiance. But the state is worthy of the kind of allegiance that calls it to deeper commitment to the will of God and love of neighbor. An allegiance that begins and ends with the state subordinates God, but an allegiance that holds the state accountable to the will and work of God is a preferred way of being a citizen of both the state and God's Kingdom.

Mahalia Jackson was likely Martin Luther King Jr.'s favorite opening act. Jackson was a gospel singer famous long before Martin Luther King gave his first Civil Rights speech. She was with Dr. King on August 23, 1963, during the March on Washington. During the long, hot day, as King was speaking, Jackson experienced a shrinking feeling. On this important day, with the rights of millions of African Americans on the line and as the world watched, King was wilting, and Jackson could sense it. The normally magnetic orator, was, like the rest of the crowd, heat-weary from a day of marching and the parade of speeches which preceded him. Sensing his speech beginning to lag, Jackson encouraged King, "Tell them about the dream, Martin."

Now one of the most famous speeches in world history, King had delivered versions of the "I Have a Dream" speech multiple times, and Mahalia Jackson figured it was time for it to be broadcast to the world. King delivered. He launched into his speech, the one which mentioned my hometown of Stone Mountain. One sentence, more than the others, speaks to the only kind of allegiance a Christ follower can faithfully offer the state. King said, "I have a dream that one day this nation will rise up and live out the true meaning of its creed: 'We hold these truths to be self-evident: that all men are created equal.'"[9]

King offered an ordered allegiance to his country, an allegiance which inspired the state not to be a great nation but to be a useful instrument of God. When Asia sat down for the Pledge in sixth grade, she knew the immensity of the sea. The rest of us were just collecting wood.

6

NATION AS NARRATIVE

Michelle Ami Reyes

On April 9, 2015, the hip-hop artist Lecrae released the music video for his song "Welcome to America." Featured on *Anomaly* and directed by Isaac Deitz, the track opens to a rising sun with a voice-over from a pilot saying, "Ladies and gentlemen / Good afternoon from the flight deck / We're cruising at thirty-seven thousand feet, and we just passed over the coast / We'll be beginning our descent in about thirty minutes / Like to take this opportunity to welcome you to America."[1] Interwoven with African chants, rhythmic drums, and a video montage of police brutality, poverty, violence, homelessness, and drugs, what follows is an electrifying and complex picture of our country's national narrative.

In rapped verse, Lecrae offers three different perspectives—from a Black drug dealer, a war veteran, and an immigrant—on the story of America and people's place in it. The poor Black man struggles to belong and is fed up with America. Nobody cares about the war veteran despite what he's done for America ("Got back and ain't nobody give a jack in America"). Perhaps in the most damning line of the song, the immigrant is told they are not wanted as the final words recount, "I couldn't get approved to stay so they sent me away from America."

Lecrae narrates these stories against the backdrop of an American flag. He references "The Star-Spangled Banner" and our country being the "land of the free, home of the brave," and at one point in the video montage we glimpse the Statue of Liberty. Through all of this, Lecrae turns our national narrative on its head, showing how the story of America is not that simple, and often we are defined as a country by who we exclude.

The profoundness of "Welcome to America" is that Lecrae, who identifies as Christian, pulls back the curtains on our American imagination, revealing that we each hold different stories of what America is and our purpose here. The artist later shares in an interview that "everyone sees [America] differently, through different lenses, and [the song] makes us take a step back and look at ourselves."[2] So, what stories have we fabricated and believed about the United States, especially as it pertains to our own mythology and ethos? How can each of us better recognize and reflect on our particular understanding of our country, our relationship to our country, and our relationship with Christ *in* our country? This chapter presents some of the myths that Americans have constructed to define the United States, both in the past and in the present, in order to help us each understand the different stories we embody and how we can work together to craft a more inclusive, multi-perspective story moving forward.

Origin Stories

Maya Angelou once said, "You can't really know where you are going until you know where you have been." People and countries alike find their identity and purpose in large part by their historical past. The past tells us where we've come from and the heroes who have paved our path, and gives meaning to the legacy we should pursue today. By definition, a nation's origin story is an inspiring narrative about that nation's past. If we want to talk about American identity, we need to go back to the beginning—to America's origin story—to understand what unique version of our nation's past we are aspiring to live into.

For most of the past four hundred years, there has been one unifying national myth, namely that the United States was founded as a Christian nation. This myth is based on what is now referred to as the Exodus story. It was first developed by historian-statesman George Bancroft in a ten-volume work entitled *History of the United States*,[3] in which he elucidates the myth as follows: In the early 1600s, English Protestants called Puritans fled the persecution and bondage of their Egypt (the Church of England and the English king) in order to venture across the wilderness (the Atlantic Ocean) and, like the Israelites before them, enter into a Promised Land (the United States). In 1620, Puritan leader William Bradford, who served as governor of the Plymouth colony settlement for many years, compared the Pilgrims' journey to the Israelites' crossing of the Sinai Desert, recorded in the book of Exodus. Upon arriving, the Puritans crafted a new covenant, a new law (American democracy) that would allow them to establish the foundations for a New Jerusalem (New England). The result of Bancroft's revisionist history was a portrait of the American experience as a cosmic drama with Christians throughout US history existing as a chosen people with a sacred mission. In this story, America is "the fulfillment of human history, the last best hope of earth."[4]

The Exodus story is based on Judeo-Christian ideas and reflects God's sovereignty and providential guidance of the Pilgrims to the land we now call the United States of America. Moreover, it sets the foundation for the belief that Christian values, institutions, and culture provided the foundation for and shaped the development of the United States. This myth is reinforced in the painting of George Washington on his knees in the snow at Valley Forge, praying to God for goodness and courage; in the religiosity of Thomas Jefferson, who drafted the Declaration of Independence; and even in Benjamin Franklin's draft seal for the United States, with the image of Moses parting the Red Sea and the Israelites crossing over behind him.[5]

These images and ideas present a religious-nationalist interpretation of American history. Our national and spiritual stories are intermingled such that our American identity is inextricable from Christianity. Fast-forward to today, within the religious-nationalist narrative, the ideal American is a God-fearing, church-attending Christian. For some of us, who grew up attending Christian schools and/or churches where both the American flag and the Christian flag hung side by side, we can easily understand how the myth of the United States as a Christian nation is a story that finds its intersection "where the flag meets the cross."[6]

The Power of National Narrative

On the one hand, the Exodus story has had a positive influence on the American imagination. The Exodus story has set the foundation for the belief that America is a great nation capable of great things. Political and religious leaders alike appeal to the religious sensibilities undergirding America's greatness when seeking to implement new projects as a nation for the common good. Dr. Martin Luther King Jr., for example, understood the ways in which America's religious-national narrative could be utilized as a positive force during the Civil Rights movement. The night before his assassination, King delivered what was to become his final sermon. Popularly titled "I've Been to the Mountaintop," King's address at Mason Temple, the Church of God in Christ headquarters, included the following lines: "I just want to do God's will. And He's allowed me to go up to the mountain.

And I've looked over. And I've seen the promised land. I may not get there with you. But I want you to know tonight, that we, as a people, will get to the promised land."[7]

In this speech, Dr. King explicitly called the United States "the promised land" and argued that pursuing equality for all is the path by which we enter the ideal state. He effectively combined Scripture with the ideals of republican democracy—equality, liberty, and pluralism, values deeply rooted in the *mythos* of the American psyche—in order to cast a moral vision that galvanized citizens to engage in radical social transformation. Helping Americans feel good about themselves as members of a Christian nation was and continues to be an effective way to empower them to live into certain national values and ideals.

The core of the Exodus story—sacrifice and freedom—has also been a powerful force to mobilize the masses in times of war. In August 2021, after the attacks of Hamid Karzai International Airport in Kabul, Afghanistan, President Biden gave a speech rife with religious national sentiment. As journalist Cara Bentley reported, "The US President said the American service members standing guard at the airport who lost their lives in the attack were heroes, part of the 'backbone' of America. He then quoted from the Old Testament to commend their eagerness to go to Afghanistan: 'Those who have served through the ages have drawn inspiration from the Book of Isaiah, when the Lord says, 'Whom shall I send . . . who shall go for us?' And the American military has been answering for a long time: 'Here am I, Lord. Send me. Here I am. Send me' [Isaiah 6:8]"[8]

Biden's statement not only shows that the religious narrative of the United States can be exploited for martial purposes—casting American soldiers as the prophet Isaiah answering God's call to serve gives a divine stamp of approval to American military exploits. It also removes any hint of wrongdoing from our collective actions as a nation. Tapping into the religious-nationalist narrative of the Exodus story, President Biden's speech affirmed the United States in a way that Americans like to be seen: as a Christian nation and a "city on a hill" in a dark world, spreading peace, freedom, and equality wherever we go.

Moreover, when Americans cling to the origin story of the United States as a Christian nation, anything non-White is seen as a threat. As professor of sociology Andrew L. Whitehead argues, the narrative of religious nationalism "really refers to a certain population, which tends to be white, native born, culturally Christian."[9] The Exodus story is grounded in a specifically White cultural framework, and this framework was constructed to give authority to Anglo-Protestant culture in the United States. Diversity, including the rise of Black and Brown leaders and new waves of immigrants, is thus viewed by many as the great weapon threatening our nation's identity. According to a joint survey by Public Religion Research and *The Atlantic*, "more than half—52 percent—of white evangelical Protestants say a majority of the U.S. population being nonwhite will be a negative development."[10]

Inherent to this belief is an unfounded fear in reverse colonization—that foreigners will come to the West and launch an anti-Christian attack. Hence why immigrants have been labeled as an "invasion" of "criminals" and "rapists,"[11] but also why Black and Brown communities are described as immoral and "rat infested," and those who care about diversity and addressing racism are described as heretics, Marxists, and liberals.[12] Inherent in their aversion to diversity is a deep-seated fear by North American White evangelicals that their story and their culture is on the verge of erasure. They believe that new voices and new stories will mean losing their own voice at the cultural and political tables—and consequently, that this will be a knock to America's greatness.

Different versions of US history that focus on the lives and experiences of racialized minorities are also seen as a danger to the religious-nationalist narrative. Demands to acknowledge the presence of indigenous peoples long before Puritans arrived on American shores—and more specifically, the genocide of indigenous nations in the pursuit of Christian expansion—are a threat to the belief in a united and unblemished nation under God. In recent years, the calls to remove Confederate statues and the launch of the 1619 Project by the *New York Times* in 2019, a long-form journalism project developed by Nikole Hannah-Jones which "aims to reframe the country's history by placing the consequences of slavery and the contributions of Black Americans at the very center of the United States' national narrative,"[13] have also challenged the depiction of our American presidents, generals, and industrial giants, even at times slaveholders, as godly Christian men who are deeply moral, even saintly, committing only minor sins and seeking to secure the greater good for our country.

The debates raging across the nation and in our schools about Critical Race Theory (CRT), a theory developed within legal studies to show how racism has shaped public policy in America, challenges the myth of "Hardworking America," in which everyone is equal, has equal access to resources and opportunities, and is capable of pulling him- or herself up by her own bootstraps.[14] From anti-immigration policies such as the Chinese Exclusion Act of 1882, to the USA PATRIOT Act by President Bush in 2001, to housing discrimination laws against racialized minorities that were only outlawed in 1968,[15] we see a different version of the past, one that flips the tables on our heroes and villains and highlights the dark stains swept under the rug of American religious exceptionalism.

The belief that the American Christian nation was under attack also played a large role in Donald Trump's successful presidential campaign. In what is now an infamous speech given at Dordt University in January 2016, Trump told a crowd of 7,600 people, "Christianity is under tremendous siege, whether we want to talk about it or we don't want to talk about it. Christians make up the overwhelming majority of the country, and yet we don't exert the power that we should have."[16] Though Trump's language lacked allusions to Scripture, he continued to hit the drum of the religious national myth in declaring that America is a Christian nation and that to "Make America Great Again," Christians must rule.

In November 2016, 56.5 percent of the country voted for Donald Trump.[17] This overwhelming support shows that Trump's words resonated with much of the American populace. According to a recent Pew Research Survey, nearly half of Americans (49 percent) think US laws should take the Bible into account at least somewhat; nearly a quarter (23 percent) of these say it should have "a great deal" of influence. Among US Christians, two-thirds (68 percent) want the Bible to influence US laws at least some. Among White evangelical Protestants, this figure rises to about nine in ten (89 percent).[18]

False Narratives

The problem is that the religious-nationalist narrative is neither accurate nor complete. The US Constitution does not mention the Bible, God, Jesus, or Christianity, and the First Amendment clarifies that "Congress shall make no law respecting an establishment of religion." Historians question the historical accuracy of George Washington's kneeling portrait, and though he supported organized religion and a higher power, Washington's personal beliefs were never fully written down and thus hard to account for.[19] Thomas Jefferson was a devout theist, who, according to some historians, "rejected the notion of the Trinity and Jesus' divinity."[20] Benjamin Franklin was in fact a deist, who believed

God created the universe but remained apart from it.[21] It would be wrong to anachronistically believe that the founding religious fathers of our country held the same beliefs and practices as White American Christians today.

Ultimately, the Exodus story is not everyone's story. When it comes to the drafting of the Constitution and America's earliest days of independence, scholars have shown that the United States was founded by a diverse group of peoples with different worldviews, values, and stories. For example, "the colony of New Netherland was established by the Dutch West India Company in 1624 and grew to encompass all of present-day New York City and parts of Long Island, Connecticut[,] and New Jersey."[22] While White Protestant men were certainly part of the original formulation of our country, other thinkers—White and Black, Jewish, Catholic, and agnostic—helped shape and reformulate it. The founding story of our country from the 1600s and 1700s is a rich mixture of Jewish, Christian, liberal, and republican peoples, ideas, and values. The United States was and always will be multicultural and multireligious.

The more we uncover US history, the greater the tear in the tapestry grows, showing that the Exodus story is incapable of unifying us (and indeed, it never fully did). The real problem is that other peoples' stories have been hidden for so long that when historians, scholars, and non-White Americans bring these details into the light, their stories are treated as bogeymen instead of what they are: the missing puzzle pieces.

What Is Our Story?

How can Americans, and American Christians in particular, work toward a more comprehensive and equitable national narrative for all? The exclusivist aspects of the core narratives that have defined the United States make clear that we need a new narrative. We need a general consensus of values and a feeling that we're part of the same long, hard, intergenerational project. Instead of one story, we need a wide range of voices contributing to a complex national narrative. That way, we can craft a big *We* that still makes space for all the little *we*s within our country.

The first step in crafting a big-tent narrative for our country involves self-assessment. Understanding our own individual journey and experiences is a crucial step before connecting the puzzle pieces for how our story fits with everyone else's. The process of recognizing and reflecting on our self-understanding through the lens of national narrative is multilayered and should hold up to the following elements: internal consistency, historical accuracy, value impact, and biblical rootedness.

1. *Internal Consistency.* Ask yourself, *Whom does my narrative include and exclude?* For example, does your story make space for how people of your own ethnic roots engaged with people of other cultures and religious beliefs? Consider who the enemies are in your story. For example, do you believe that illegal immigrants are

the greatest threat to America? Conversely, have you labeled all White people as the enemy?

2. *Historical Accuracy.* Ask yourself, *Does the story of America that I believe in give a defensible history of the nation's history?* Consider who the main historical players (past and present) are in your version of a national narrative. What are the achievements of your historical heroes? Have scholars verified or debunked these claims? Assessing the historical accuracy of our national stories requires time and research as we move from simply receiving "truths" passed down to us and begin to study, question, and analyze the information for ourselves.

3. *Value Impact.* Ask yourself, *What do I value above all else as an American? How do these values either help or harm other people?* For example, does your national story lead to justification of violence or intolerance? We all need to face our moral failures, individually and as a country. American sociologist Philip Gorski writes, "We should be careful not to imagine that we are always on the right side of history all of the time. The line between good and evil does not run between people, but through them."[23]

4. *Biblical Assessment.* Finally, ask yourself, *Does my story and the subsequent way I live my life (e.g., my political views) align with Scripture's call to love God and love*

my neighbor? The Bible says that we must "demolish arguments and every pretension that sets itself up against the knowledge of God" and "take captive every thought to make it obedient to Christ" (2 Corinthians 10:5). This means that we must bring every story in our lives before the Lord in prayer, asking for his Spirit to give us discernment on whether these stories—and their present-day ramifications—glorify God.

The second step is to challenge ourselves to better see, hear, and make space for the stories of our neighbors. We need to take time to sit down and learn each other's stories and, more importantly, allow each other's narratives and identities to have room to breathe and flourish. This includes creating a more robust political vocabulary (using the terms and definitions included in this chapter and others that prove helpful) to enable dialogue and healthy debate between people with differing views of our country and its purpose in the world. It also means that as we pursue a more multicultural version of a national narrative, we embrace our unique cultural roots and ethnic heritages without disassociating ourselves from our fellow Americans, whether they are Black, White, or Brown.

Our third and final step is to pursue a path forward that involves compromise. We need to value alliances when it comes to an American national identity. The United States can neither be a country of apocalyptic religion and imperial zeal nor be a blend of cultural elitism. It has never been (nor ever will be) a wholly Christian nation or the offspring of an entirely secularized and fractured multicultural project. It has never been the story of one people group either. Our story should not cause us to participate in national self-worship or self-loathing. Each of these are extremes, lacking nuance and full representation of the American people. What we need instead is a national story born from a spirit of ecumenism, generosity, and civic friendship in which Brown, Black, and White, men, women, and children can flourish together. Compromise means asking questions such as "In what ways are each of our narratives committed to liberty, equality, and the pursuit of happiness?"

As American Christians, we need to make space in our national narrative for an all-encompassing tent where we can still be true to our religious beliefs, and in which we can value American culture and institutions enough to cherish them while not succumbing to the belief that America is always a force for good in the world. I cannot tell you what this compromise should look like specifically. That would defeat the purpose of dialogue. But if we can open ourselves to these forms of self-assessment and engagement, we will be on a stabler path to finding unity as a nation and within the story we are living in, even in times of deep division like the present.

7

STRANGERS IN
A STRANGE LAND

Tina Boesch

SNAPPING A PASSPORT PHOTO OF A ONE-WEEK-OLD INFANT is more difficult than you would imagine. As my husband and I discovered to our dismay, the requirement that both eyes be open in a passport photo applies to babies as well as adults. But in the first week of life, while newborns are still recovering from the trauma of delivery, they're champion sleepers. Take my word for it: Coaxing an infant to open her eyes long enough to snap a photo with adequate light and her head perfectly positioned for the camera requires preternatural patience and pyrotechnics.

The first outing we took with each of our three children after their births was to the US Consulate. We waited with our swaddled newborn in a line outside an imposing government compound with a completed application form in hand. Four neatly clipped square photos of an infant squinting miserably into the light of an incomprehensible new reality were victoriously clipped to the top left corner.

All three of our kids are American citizens born abroad— one in Cyprus and two in Turkey. People often ask if that means they're dual citizens. The answer is a regrettable no. There are benefits of citizenship for certain—the right of residence, protections of the law, government services and education only available to citizens. But citizenship carries civic responsibilities as well as rights. In Turkey, for instance, male citizens are obligated to serve in the military. As much as we wanted our son to identify with the country in which he was born, we also wanted to spare him the obligation of military service. Since they were not citizens of Turkey, our kids were considered *yabancı*, a Turkish word that means foreigner.

The word *yabancı* is flexible depending on context. It can mean that someone is not a citizen, or it can be used to describe someone who's a stranger. It's the word of choice when someone is unknown or perceived as an outsider. It can be applied to people who don't belong and aren't understood. Most often, it's used to label foreigners who aren't Turkish, who visit the country as tourists, reside there temporarily for work, or flee to it as refugees. For the fourteen years we lived in Turkey, we were always *yabancı*. We were noncitizens, *strangers*.

The condition of being a stranger should not be strange to a Christian. After all, from the moment God called a man named Abram to uproot himself from the place he belonged—to leave his country, his kindred, and his father's house to journey to the land that God would show him—the people of God have been marked as *yabancı*, strangers on the move (Genesis 12:1-4). Centuries after Abram struck out in obedience to the divine summons, God prepared his descendants to enter into the land promised to their forefather by reminding them, "The land shall not be sold in perpetuity for the land is mine. *For you are strangers and sojourners with me*" (Leviticus 25:23, ESV, emphasis added). God reinforced the truth that the identity of his people would be found in their relationship with him, not in the physical borders of the country in which they reside.

This is a theme developed by the writer of Hebrews, who reminds us that Abram, the father of faith, retained the identity as a foreigner even after he had arrived in the land of promise: "By faith he stayed *as a foreigner* in the land of promise, living in tents as did Isaac and Jacob, coheirs of the same promise. For he was looking forward to the city that has foundations, whose architect and builder is God" (Hebrews 11:9-10, CSB, emphasis added). Even when he had pitched his tent in the promised land of Canaan, Abram was a *yabancı*, a foreigner, because his citizenship rested in God's eternal Kingdom. And so it is with all people who follow the God of Abram, Isaac, and Jacob. In trusting God's promise, they "confessed that they were *foreigners* and temporary residents on the earth" who are seeking an eternal homeland (Hebrews 11:13, CSB, emphasis added).

In his teaching ministry Jesus often sketched the contours of that eternal homeland—the Kingdom of God—with parables at once mystifying and clarifying. He labored diligently to distinguish between the Kingdom of God and the kingdoms of this world, between the way of living characteristic of citizens of God's Kingdom and the behaviors and values endemic in the world. "I bestow on you a kingdom," Jesus promised (Luke 22:29, CSB), "but that kingdom *is not like the kingdoms of this world*" (John 18:36, author's paraphrase). "The phrase 'kingdom of heaven,'" N. T. Wright reminds us, "does not refer to a place, called 'heaven,' where God's people will go after death. It refers to the rule of heaven, that is, of God being brought to bear in the present world."[1] And that rule—God's standard for a way of being that promotes human flourishing—is brought to bear by the people who have heard and responded to the call to repent, believe, and follow Jesus, while loving God with their whole hearts, minds, and souls and their neighbors as themselves.

As citizens of God's Kingdom, there's a sense in which we become strangers and exiles within our home country. Abundant, flourishing lives should be a hallmark of the presence of Christian strangers in the world, but two temptations can mar our mission. Let's highlight the temptations we must wrestle with before turning to the opportunities for us as strangers.

The Temptations of Being a Stranger:
Dominion and Disengagement

While I was scrolling through my newsfeed this morning, a devastating headline caught my attention.[2] More than two hundred bodies of children, some as young as three years old, were found at the Kamloops Indian Residential School, a state-funded Christian school in Canada. From the 1800s to the 1970s, First Nations parents were forced to surrender their children into the "care" of these schools "as part of a program to assimilate them into Canadian society," a program which meant stripping them of their cultural heritage and isolating them from their bereft families. Among other things, education meant compulsory conversion to Christianity. While at the Kamloops Indian Residential School, children were "not allowed to speak their native languages," and "many were beaten and verbally abused." Across Canada thousands of children died from maltreatment in residential schools like Kamloops.

Reports of tragedies like this one confirm the fear that when Christian strangers occupy a new land, they come to dominate. The temptation to cultural domination may not be unique to Christianity, but it has been a besetting one for Western expressions of Christianity, particularly in the era of colonialism, when military might, economic interest, and missionary endeavors blended into a bitter cocktail. When Christian strangers find themselves in a strange land, they're called to the ministry of reconciliation, not dominion. As

Kevin Vanhoozer puts it, "The church's mission is to present Christ, not to extend Christendom."[3]

It was, in fact, missionaries themselves who emerged among the most vocal critics of dominionist and colonial tendencies. Roland Allen, who served in China in the late nineteenth century, offered a blistering critique of European mission compounds removed from local communities and missionaries who weren't versed in local cultural expressions and norms. Allen's writings inspired a wholesale re-evaluation of missionary methods,[4] a renewed respect for indigenous cultures, and an awareness that as Christ's church takes root in new cultures, it must do so within the local idiom, culture, and life of the people. Christians who blend the gospel with the preferences and trappings of their own culture run the risk of championing the values of the kingdoms of this world while obscuring the identity of Jesus, who established a different sort of Kingdom.

If dominion is one temptation citizens of Christ's Kingdom must wrestle against, its counterpart is disengagement. While some Christians may be tempted to take over, others are tempted to withdraw from civic responsibility altogether, establishing insular communities with little to no regard for the concerns and needs of those with whom they don't share common beliefs. Disengagement is the disposition of the priest and the teacher of the law in Jesus' parable of the Good Samaritan, two religious leaders who walked by a suffering neighbor because they felt absolved of responsibility for anyone outside their own community of faith. Underlying both

these unholy orientations—dominion and disengagement—
is a sense of superiority that Jesus consistently opposed in
both his teaching and practice.

I confess that disengagement is more a temptation to me
than dominion. From our vantage point in the twenty-first
century, disengagement may seem like a necessary correc-
tive to the excessive confidence of the colonial era, when
European cultural norms were often seen as an essential
aspect of faithful Christian expression. But disengagement
can lead to a secretive faith. In the interest of not imposing my Christian beliefs on others, I may be tempted not
to express them at all. But if I truly believe that abundant
life, forgiveness, freedom, and restoration are found in Christ
alone, then silence in the presence of those who do not yet
know him is neither respectful nor loving.

While thinking about these fraternal-twin temptations of
dominion and disengagement, I've been reading Atossa Araxia
Abrahamian's book, *The Cosmopolites: The Coming of the
Global Citizen.* The idea of becoming a "global citizen" carries
with it the allure of freedom of travel and the aura of respect
for many cultures. As someone who has matured through
travel and participation with churches in many cultures, the
idea of identifying as a "global Christian" appeals to me. But
reading Abrahamian's account of the way the ultrawealthy
have used the category of global citizen to avoid local civic
responsibilities has prompted me to see that in some cases,
the globalization of identity (and in the Christian context, the
globalization of our faith) can mask a form of disengagement.

In 2011 when Facebook cofounder Eduardo Saverin renounced his American citizenship to defect to Singapore just prior to his company's initial public offering, it's probable the absence of capital-gains taxes was more of a motivator than a love of South Asian culture. Abrahamian wryly comments that Saverin's "global, a la carte approach to citizenship, residence, and taxation flies in the face of a more traditional view of belonging, which entails lifelong rights and responsibilities."[5] The value of local citizenship may be shrugged off by those who don't want to bear the responsibilities of it, but that self-centered approach doesn't promote healthy community or the flourishing of our neighbors.

Christians dwell in a tension between the recognition that the church transcends political borders, and the witness of the life of the body of believers, which demonstrates that discipleship must be expressed in the context of local communities. Miriam Adeney, author of *Kingdom Without Borders* and a vocal advocate for the international church, cautions against disengagement from local expressions of the body of Christ:

> Being a world citizen is too vague to provide motivation and meaning. It makes the common person feel insignificant. On the other hand, if you are a member of a distinct culture or local group, you have celebrations which give zest, values which give a cognitive framework, action patterns which give direction to your days, and associational ties

which root you in a human context. You have a place in time in the universe, a base for the conviction that you are part of the community of life flowing from the past and pulsing on into the future. *You have a story.*[6]

You have a story. As the people who walk in the Way of Jesus, we've entered a story that began many millennia ago in a garden where Adam and Eve walked with God in the cool of the day, a story that reached its climax when God sent his Son to redeem and restore the relationships that our sinful rebellion against his rule destroyed. But we're also participants in the story of the communities in which we live. In his letter to the church at Philippi, Paul encourages, "As citizens of heaven, live your life worthy of the gospel of Christ. Then, whether I come and see you or am absent, I will hear about you that you are standing firm in one spirit, in one accord, contending together for the faith of the gospel" (Philippians 1:27, CSB).

Paul called the Philippian believers to live within their city in a manner worthy of the gospel. As Christians we don't relinquish the responsibilities we have to our own communities or the nation in which we're citizens because we enter God's Kingdom; rather, our responsibilities are amplified because we become ambassadors for an eternal Kingdom within our temporal home. The challenge is to take God's story with us into the cultures, countries, towns, neighborhoods, and subcultures where we're called to plant our lives and raise our families, translating it into the local idioms of rural Appalachia or inner-city Chicago, of Portland or New Orleans, of Kyoto, Kuala Lumpur, or Kandahar.

The Opportunities of Being a Stranger: Translation and Perspective

One of the most wonderful things about meeting a stranger is the chance to hear a new set of stories. But before a stranger can recount a compelling story, she must learn the language of the people with whom she wants to communicate. Among the myriad tragedies of the approach to evangelism at the Kamloops Indian Residential school was that Christian teachers forced First Nations children to learn English rather than translating the story of God's redemptive work through Christ into their own native tongue. That approach runs counter to the spirit of Pentecost, a seminal moment in the birth of the church, when a crowd of Parthians, Medes, Elamites, Mesopotamians, Cappadocians, Cretans, Egyptians, Libyans, and Arabs all heard Galilean followers of Jesus speaking of "the mighty works of God" in their own native languages (Acts 2:5-11, esv).

Ever since the disorienting, electrifying experience of Pentecost, Christians have been translating the mighty works of God into the languages of the peoples of the world. Fulfilling Christ's commission to make disciples of every nation, baptizing them in the name of the Father, Son, and Spirit and teaching them to obey all that he commanded ultimately depends on the facility with which Christians are able to communicate clearly and winsomely in local, vernacular languages—the heart languages that people use in their homes and for their most intimate conversations.

Christians are first and foremost translators. We translate the story of God's work in the world, of his self-revelation through time, of his incarnation in Christ, and of Jesus' victory over sin and death into a language the people with whom we live, work, and play can understand. And we translate it by living it out in relationships, so that others can grasp the goodness of the life Jesus came to establish. And that means that as citizens of Jesus' Kingdom, we can't keep our strangeness private in the public sphere.

In *Translating the Message*, Lamin Sanneh observed, "The language question lies at the very heart of the Christian movement."[7] In the early centuries of the growth of the church, Hebrew and Greek Scriptures were translated into Latin, Coptic, Syriac, and Armenian. A scholar born in the Gambia, Sanneh has forced a re-evaluation of the impact of the spread of Christianity on indigenous cultures. Counter to the claim that Christians destroy culture, Sanneh believed that "missionaries shielded indigenous cultures from Western intellectual domination."[8] His conclusion flows from the reality that the efforts of Bible translators around the world have protected indigenous languages from extinction and have highlighted the value and beauty of vernacular languages. In cultures where Christian strangers painstakingly labored to adopt terms and concepts meaningful in local cultures and used them to express truth revealed in the Bible, their efforts stimulated cultural renewal. Bible translation into minority and tribal languages demonstrates that the goodness of the gospel is not just for elites who master trade languages, it's for villagers, mothers, fishermen, and bakers.

There have been many moments in the long history of the church when Christians have lived into the hard and holy calling to communicate Christ while resisting the temptations of dominion and disengagement. I think, for instance, of Lilias Trotter, who forfeited her comfortable life in England and the potential of a luminous career as a painter to make her home in Algiers, living among Muslims.[9] From her base at Dar Naama in Algeria, Lilias oversaw the translation of the Gospel of John. Reflecting on that work, she observed, "It is not the question of just giving a gospel of words that the people can understand, but to give them the germ of a spiritual language in which the things that the Holy Ghost teaches can be expressed—the dearth of it seems in the inverse ratio to the richness of the tongue for all secular purposes."[10]

In 1917 during a two-month trip south from Tunis to Tozeur, Lilias connected with members of a Sufi brotherhood, a mystic sect of Islam. She began visiting frequently and her bond with the Sufis grew strong. "'She knows about The Way,' they would say of her."[11] After more than three decades in North Africa, she began composing a book for her Sufi friends on the seven "I am" statements of Christ. Taking as her starting point the seven most profound Sufi longings, Lilias demonstrated how Jesus fulfilled them all as the

Bread, the Light, the Door, the Shepherd, the Resurrection and Life, the Way, and the Vine. Grounded in the Gospel of John, Lilias's writing in *The Sevenfold Secret* translated Jesus' self-revelation for the Sufis, connecting biblical truth to the longing of their souls. Later, Harold Stalley, who continued her ministry to the brotherhood, said the Sufis repeatedly commented, "This is *our* book."[12]

It takes Christian strangers to translate the message of the gospel for people living in cultures where it hasn't yet been clearly expressed. Those who faithfully translate the Good News often discover that their immersion in cultural contexts different from the one in which they were raised refines their own understanding of the Good News. And this leads us to our second opportunity as strangers living in strange lands—clarifying perspective. Lesslie Newbigin, a British pastor who served among Christians in India, testifies to the illuminating nature of living as a stranger in *The Open Secret*: "I have to bear witness that the experience of living for most of four decades as part of an Indian church has made me acutely aware of the cultural conditioning of the Christianity in which I was nurtured, and of the culture-bound character of many of the assumptions that are unquestioned by English Christians."[13] When Newbigin returned to England after nearly half a century in India, he found that he had become a stranger in his home culture. It was precisely a perspective from outside his country of citizenship that enabled him to speak so presciently to the secularism that had quietly colonized the faith of many

Western Christians in his book *Foolishness to the Greeks: The Gospel and Western Culture.*

The perspective gained from embracing our status as strangers in this world has the potential to instill a deep humility tied to the recognition that no local, temporal church will ever perfectly embody the principles of the Kingdom Jesus established until he returns to restore all things. As Newbigin puts it, "The church is in the world as the place where Jesus, in whom all the fullness of the godhead dwells, is present, but it is not itself that fullness. It is the place where the filling is taking place (Eph. 1:23)."[14]

In my years living as a stranger in Turkey, I often discovered how impoverished my understanding of aspects of Christian discipleship were because they had been shaped primarily by my American cultural context. For instance, I don't think I fully understood the sacrificial nature of hospitality until one summer when we were driving toward the Aegean Sea for a short vacation. The engine light on our van lit up, so we called a Turkish friend in a nearby town to ask if she could recommend a mechanic. She met us for lunch, picked up the tab for all seven of us, and then led us to the mechanic with whom she and her husband had arranged to pay for our repairs. Because we were guests in their city, she insisted that we stay in her home. During the overnight visit, their entire family slept on couches downstairs so that we could stay in the most comfortable rooms. The sacrificial nature of my Turkish friends' hospitality challenged my own notions of generosity, of welcoming strangers, and of honoring those who go out "for the sake of the Name" (3 John 1:5-8).

From *Yabancı* to *Kardeş*

Remember the Turkish word *yabancı*? For all the years we lived in Turkey, we were *yabancı*, foreigners. And yet we found that our Turkish neighbors and friends affectionately referred to us as *kardeş*—as *siblings*, not strangers. My downstairs neighbor was our *teyze*, our auntie; my friend Aysel was my kids' *abla*, their big sister. On the playground, mothers would introduce their children to my kids by referring to them not as *yabancı* but as *kardeş*. These terms of endearment are used to describe intimate family relationships, and they're often extended to include others who are known, accepted, and loved. These familiar names gave my kids a sense of belonging and safety in a land that was not officially their country of citizenship.

In Ephesians 2:12-19, Paul reminds us that we were once "excluded from the citizenship of Israel, and foreigners to the covenants of promise." But in Christ, "*you are no longer foreigners and strangers*, but fellow citizens with the saints, and members of God's household" (CSB, emphasis added). In Christ, we're *kardeş*, brothers and sisters, members of one family. And our mission on this wild and wonderful earth is to welcome others into the household of faith by treating them as *kardeş*, as siblings. We serve, we forgive, we love unconditionally, we bind up wounds, we pray for those who persecute because we're called to a way of being that reflects the character of Jesus, whose Kingdom will never end. We find ourselves living into Jesus' parable of the great banquet in Luke 14:15-24. We're transformed into the servants sent by the master into the street and lanes in the area to coax as many people as possible to come to the feast.

MY FELLOW CITIZENS

Alejandro Mandes

*I, therefore, the prisoner of the Lord, beseech you to walk worthy of the
calling with which you were called, with all lowliness and gentleness, with
longsuffering, bearing with one another in love, endeavoring to keep the unity
of the Spirit in the bond of peace. There is one body and one Spirit, just as
you were called in one hope of your calling; one Lord, one faith, one baptism;
one God and Father of all, who is above all, and through all, and in you all.*

EPHESIANS 4:1-6, NKJV

*The road is long and weary. Sometimes my brother
carries me, and sometimes I carry him.*

SALVADOR DE LUNA

TODAY WE WHO ARE DISCIPLES OF THE LORD JESUS CHRIST
live in an exciting transitional time where we are watching
a different America being birthed right before our eyes.[1] I
call it the New Samaria,[2] which is partially the result of a
vast demographic shift. In the last few decades, the bulk of
population growth in the United States has been the result of
continued increases among multiracial, Asian, and Hispanic

populations. According to US Census predictions, the US will become majority nonwhite by 2045.[3] This change is not stopping and cannot be dismissed by vote or religious resolutions.

In other words, those whom the majority culture has historically thought of as "other" are now part of "us." Those people on the other side of our walls, our political parties, and our ideologies? They are our neighbors, our brothers and sisters, our fellow image-bearers of God. We are commanded to love one another. And to love one another, we need to listen to and learn from each other, to learn to see with each other's eyes.

As a Hispanic who grew up speaking Spanish, then English, raised in Laredo on the Texas side of the US-Mexico border, I know the life of an outsider. I experienced culture clash when educated in Austin and Dallas, and I have lived the life of cultural roadkill. Now, as a follower of Christ who leads the segment in our denominational ministry that works with people in the margins of society, I am constantly in public discourse with people over issues of cultural engagement. I would be lying if I said it doesn't hurt sometimes, but I have learned to benefit and grow from this discussion.

The Call to Become Citizen-Disciples

In the passage cited at the start of this chapter, the apostle Paul called for all disciples to seek the unity of the Spirit. The term I use for this in the context of cultural engagement is "citizen-disciples"—men and women who are less issue-oriented and more Kingdom-minded on eternal realities based on God's mandates.

The call of a citizen-disciple is dual citizenship: seeking the Kingdom on earth now and preparing for the Kingdom to come. It is a call to the Great Commandment of love, united to the Great Commission of making disciples of all people, that will result in the Great Community. The Great Community is the local church that lives out its transformation and impacts the neighborhood so that the neighborhood around the church perceives the fragrance of Christ.

The citizen-disciple is called to unity on essentials but charity in difference. This unity requires cultural humility because we have to open our eyes to see the harvest long in coming but often ignored.[4] This is hard work because this call to unity, if obeyed, will result in the breaking of some and the freeing of others to engage the New Samaria now asserting itself in America and being mirrored in many countries around the world.

In essence, these are the birthing contractions of a new reality. This rebirth can be painful, but pain can be a great teacher, telling us that something significant is happening. The child being born is a diverse church unified in faith, and I believe the birthing pains will be forgotten when we see the beautiful, unified church that emerges from our hard work.

Let me be very clear: I love America, with my eyes wide open. I have traveled enough to know America has deep faults, but I also know that Christianity has been the basis for much of the good in our land. As a student of history, I also know that as a nation and a church, we have not lived up to our words. And I know that at times I have not lived up to my own desires as a disciple. We can do better!

As a fellow sojourner, I therefore submit the following thoughts to help us move toward a unified church as fellow citizen-disciples to reach the hope of unity in God's beautifully diverse garden, here and now.

Principles for Citizen-Disciples

I believe that the rebirth process for the citizen-disciple begins with a reorientation around several biblical principles.

We Are All Made in God's Image

We must humbly recognize that every person we encounter is made in the image of God (Genesis 1:26). Consider a conversation between our Lord and the Pharisees. The presenting question was about paying taxes. Jesus asked to see a coin.

> [Jesus] said to them, "Whose image and inscription is this?" They said to him, "Caesar's."
>
> And Jesus answered and said to them, "Render to Caesar the things that are Caesar's, and to God the things that are God's."
>
> MARK 12:16-17, NKJV

This was meant to be a trick question by the Pharisees about who had authority to tax and control. Jesus' answer was profound. Essentially, Jesus said that whoever's image is on an item is its owner. It was easy enough for the questioner to understand that the taxes should be paid to Caesar because Caesar's image was on the coin. The unstated corollary was that people are made in God's image and thus belong to God. The Pharisees thought the conversation would be about taxes, but Jesus made it about ownership. The image of God is on every human being, and they belong to him. As C. S. Lewis put it ever so eloquently:

> It is a serious thing to live in a society of possible gods and goddesses, to remember that the dullest and most uninteresting person you can talk to may one day be a creature which, if you say it now, you would be strongly tempted to worship, or else a horror and a corruption such as you now meet, if at all, only in a nightmare. . . . And our charity must be a real and costly love, with deep feeling for the sins in spite of which we love the sinner—no mere tolerance, or indulgence which parodies love as flippancy parodies merriment.[5]

When we are in the middle of a public discourse and tempted to label, blame, and dismiss, we must remember that we speak to fellow image-bearers. This, at the very least, should slow us down from being dismissive. This does not mean that we must agree with each other's counterpoint, but it does mean that the other person should be respected and listened to carefully, if for no other reason because they are made in the image of God.

God Desires Unity in the Midst of Diversity

Even before choosing the Jews as his people to demonstrate his relationship with humans, God declared his desire to be a blessing to the whole world when he promised Abraham that all families of the earth would be blessed through him (Genesis 12:3). Then, as Paul points out in Ephesians 2, the death of Christ destroyed the ages-old wall separating Jews and Gentiles:

> He Himself is our peace, who has made both [Jews and Gentiles] one, and has broken down the middle wall of separation, having abolished in His flesh the enmity, that is, the law of commandments contained in ordinances, so as to create in Himself one new man from the two, thus making peace, and that He might reconcile them both to God in one body through the cross, thereby putting to death the enmity. And He came and preached peace to you who were afar off and to those who were near. For through Him we both have access by one Spirit to the Father.
>
> EPHESIANS 2:14-18, NKJV

Until Jesus brought down the wall of separation, the Jews lived as if they were the only people of God. Jews who were

viewed as being defiled by Hellenistic culture were persecuted. The Gentiles living in Samaria, like the woman at the
well, were loathed even more. This disdain was genuine, even
though the Scriptures gave many hints that God's ultimate
intention was one family of all people.

The Gospels are full of examples of Jesus relating to
Gentiles. Jesus was raised among the Gentiles in Galilee. He
spent time in the non-Jewish regions around Galilee, including Perea, which is the Transjordan; the Decapolis, a league
of ten Greco-Roman cities; Samaria; and many other Gentile
areas. Jesus loved being among the diversity of his creation.
Many of the most loved and used stories in the Bible happened among these marginalized people. They were even held
up as examples, such as in the story of the Good Samaritan
(Luke 10:25-37) and the account of the woman at the well
(John 4:4-42). Jesus didn't just destroy the wall of separation
by his death; he loved being among marginalized people during his earthly life. He went out of his way to be among them,
showing us by example that God's desire is unity.

Unity Draws Spiritual Warfare

In the book of Ephesians, the apostle Paul lays out a theological vision for the composition of the church:

- Chapter 2 talks about our salvation.
- Chapter 3 talks about the church united.
- Chapters 4–5 talk about walking in unity and love
  in relationships.

After those profound topics are expounded, one might expect a proclamation of celebration. Instead, Paul lays out the tools necessary for spiritual warfare. Nothing is so fragile as unity among God's people, and there are almost unlimited ways to spoil this delicate gift of God. Something so precious is worth fighting for, but the fight for this unity is not waged with guns and bombs. The weapons are truth, righteousness, peace, faith, prayer, and watchfulness (Ephesians 6:14-18).

Who is the enemy? More often than not, it can be God's people who are duped into living selfishly and self-righteously. Sometimes instead of living out the Great Commission, we exercise the Great Omission, failing to love our neighbors. Instead of standing against evil, we simply don't stand. Satan does not need to enter humanity to destroy the great work of God. We all are more than able and willing to be his servants. As citizen-disciples, we should remain watchful for supernatural division around and through us.

Practices of Citizen-Disciples

In addition to reorienting our perspective, there are many practices that can help citizen-disciples press toward unity.

Recognize Our Diverse Reality

The first important practice for citizen-disciples is to open our eyes to see today's diverse reality. Defining reality involves looking at what is really happening in our community and our country, rather than expecting reality to conform to our perception of how things were or should be. Some who pine for the simple days of the past may have a selective memory. And in the present, changing cultural and demographic realities are easily dismissed or left to the next generation to engage.

To silence the dissonance of the day, we withdraw into personal castles, where we control the drawbridge. We often do not want to hear anything that threatens our personal peace and prosperity. We quibble about words that relieve us of God's inconvenient mandate to love our neighbor, and we try to ignore the pain we see on our screens. We will surrender anything bit by bit so that our personal peace and prosperity are not bothered. In the end, however, the walls we create blind us to the reality of the mission field materializing before us. If we want to define reality, citizen-disciples must let down the drawbridge of our castles and open our eyes to see the reality of our changing landscape.

Open Ourselves to Different Points of View

We who are citizen-disciples must approach different points of view with open eyes, ears, and hearts. The story of the woman at the well in John 4 is a study in cultural blinders because the Jews did not want to see what Jesus saw as a mission field. And when we look at the book of Acts, the reality is that the people in the margins, the Gentiles, extended Christ's mission:

- The Hellenistic Jews were marginalized by the Hebraic majority in Jerusalem. They complained to the apostles, who listened to the injustice and empowered them to make things right. The Hellenistic deacons responded by feeding all widows (Acts 6).

- After the persecution began following Stephen's stoning, the Hebraic Jews evangelized the Jews while the Hellenistic Jews evangelized the Gentiles (Acts 8).

- The first Gentile church in Antioch became the church that heard the call of the Holy Spirit to reach the world (Acts 13).

Jesus' challenge to the disciples—"Open your eyes and look at the fields! They are ripe for harvest" (John 4:35)—should challenge all of us as followers of Christ. As citizen-disciples, we should ask ourselves: *Am I seeing what God sees? What personal biases prevent me from seeing what God sees?*

Remove Barriers to Conversation

There are all kinds of barriers of our own making, including physical and virtual walls, that create obstacles to open dialogue. In 2021 I went to McAllen, Texas, to attend the high-school graduation of my brother's children. It was especially important because my brother had died just the year before, and I wanted to be there for them. During one stretch of the trip, we drove alongside a massive, rust-colored wall built to keep illegal immigrants from entering the country. This border wall has become the symbol of so much fighting between proponents of differing visions of America.

Walls are not always physical; sometimes they are virtual. In Acts 6, we see the early-church widows divided into groups of Greeks and Hebrews. In church history, men of God burned each other over a fire over whether someone was an Arminian or a Calvinist. People in the same church will fight over politics. People will even fight over physical features that individuals have no control over, such as skin color, gender, and generation.

The problem with walls is that they limit our ability to see the mission of God. Citizen-disciples will therefore seek to tear down walls, rather than build more of them.

Be Quick to Listen

I am not by nature a good listener, so listening has become an acquired skill. I am wired to walk into a room with my mouth first. My tendency contrasts with the counsel I received from a friend who is a communications expert. When I first met her at the Multi-Ethnic Conference several years ago, I asked if she could give me a quick communications tip. She said that the first and most important tip that she shares in her workshops is that people must first "shut up." After hearing this comment, I tried several times to work up a rebuttal, but every time I realized any retort would validate her point.

I mulled over James 1:19, which I had memorized long ago: "Everyone should be quick to listen, slow to speak and slow to become angry." Unfortunately, in this fast-paced world, we are too quick to want to know whose side people are on to reduce them to a category of thought instead of taking the time to listen, understand, and process our thoughts.

Believe it or not, many disagreements can be assuaged just by *really* listening. Citizen-disciples approach discussions with civility, kindness, and a heart to appreciate other people's points of view.

Remain Rooted in Scripture

Citizen-disciples must be rooted in the eternal Scriptures, not in constantly shifting human laws and cultural drifts. We are here for just a season, but the word of God stands forever (1 Peter 1:25). I am not minimizing the importance of law and culture as much as elevating the unchanging word of God. Sometimes it seems that we seek silos and echo chambers that validate our beliefs and fears, rather than engage with other committed disciples in fruitful conversations, seeking to understand God's word in this day.

It is only as we break down our silos, respectfully listening together for God's will, that we will have a chance to distance ourselves from the selfish chatter of the world. Citizen-disciples do not use the Bible as a rock to beat someone. They make the word of God their citizens' guide, living out the Bible even before people hear it from their mouths.

A Final Charge to Citizen-Disciples

In 2019 I went with eighteen national leaders to the National Memorial for Peace and Justice (aka the "lynching museum") in Montgomery, Alabama. Fifteen were Caucasian; three were African American; plus me. It was the most painful thing I have ever witnessed as we walked into the past and saw the photos and read the placards describing the historical justification for such inhumanity. I felt the pain that our African American brothers and sisters have had to endure over the centuries. Frankly, the same could have been shared by many other marginalized groups.

These pains were not just inflicted by haters; they also came from supposed God-fearing men and women. Denominations and Christian leaders justified them. But, since the vulnerable were the minority, they were not able to tell their stories. My question, over and over, was *Where was the church?* Indeed, some good men and women stood for the vulnerable. I remember writing in my diary that I would personally carry the pain of my brothers and sisters as my own pain from that day on.

I decided that I would not condemn the people who perpetrated these sins but would do everything to help my generation live as citizen-disciples who own and learn from the past. Let us accept the intention of our Lord to be a church united. We cannot agree to this by might, right, or fright. Our unity, the unity that can accomplish the mission of God, must come from a denial of our rights, not relying on any entitled majority position or a minority attitude that "it is not our turn." We must do this significant work by yielding to the power of the Holy Spirit and walking together. We need each other even in times of pain.

I love art because sometimes it can better say what

I struggle to explain. Sometimes art also does a great job of articulating the heart of God. The title of a song from the 1970s says it best for me: "He Ain't Heavy, He's My Brother."[6] I hope I am not alone in believing that these days are exciting. We will only succeed as citizen-disciples who declare, "He ain't heavy, he is my brother" or "She ain't heavy, she is my sister."

El es mi hermano.

Yeye sio mzito ni ndugu yangu.

그는 무겁지 않고 내 동생입니다.

9

POLITICS, PULPIT, AND PEW

Juliet Liu

In late January of 2017, President Trump signed Executive Order 13769, an order which denied the entry of travelers from seven Muslim nations into the United States, ceased the acceptance of Syrian war refugees, and drastically decreased the overall number of refugees granted entry into the United States. In response to this executive order, which came to be known as "the Muslim ban," a substantial number of well-known evangelical leaders penned an open letter published by the *Washington Post* to voice criticism of the president's actions: "As Christians, we have a historic call expressed over two thousand years to serve the suffering. We cannot abandon this call now."[1] Yet while most prominent evangelical leaders opposed President Trump's measures, according to a study by Pew Research at the time, 76 percent of white evangelicals voiced agreement with the president's executive order. In her book *The Liturgy of Politics*, Kaitlyn Schiess argues that this significant disparity between the reaction of American evangelical *leaders* and American evangelicals at the *grassroots level* revealed a surprising gap between the convictions of evangelical leaders and the people they led. This "gap" was a wake-up call to church leaders about how powerfully formed the people in our pews are by surrounding political forces.[2]

For some Christian leaders, avoiding politics seems like the better option to getting swept up in the influence of corrupted earthly power structures or becoming partisan lackeys. Yet the question must be raised: Are we being faithful shepherds in steering clear of politics altogether? As Schiess writes, many evangelical leaders who follow the guidance to stay away from politics in their preaching and teaching end up with parishioners whose faith is "not apolitical, just *unexamined*."[3]

Not apolitical, just *unexamined*. In other words, is it possible that in steering clear of politics, we have abdicated our authority to spiritually nurture and disciple the Christians in our churches in the ways they navigate politics? In the absence of intentional and thoughtful political discipleship, Christians in our congregations are being formed instead by the hostile and ubiquitous partisan voices that surround them, vying for their allegiance. When pastors and faith leaders stay silent on political issues, the rest of the church is left without the wisdom, knowledge, or tools to discern political engagement. They are like sheep without a shepherd.

So, what does intentional discipleship look like regarding politics and the church—and what is required from both the pulpit and the pew for that discipleship to happen?

From the Pulpit: Preach the Gospel, Pastors!

"Just preach the gospel; no need to get political, pastor." It's not an uncommon statement I have heard from various persons with good intentions, from my homiletics professor in seminary to an older, White gentleman in my congregation who wanted to offer me feedback on my preaching over breakfast. My honest question in response is always, "What do you mean when you say, 'Preach the gospel'? How do *you* understand the gospel?"

I prayed the believer's prayer for the first time at the age of fifteen in a crowded yet spacious Southern Baptist sanctuary, and nearly every Sunday after that before going to college. The gospel story I heard preached was straightforward and demanded an urgent response: Jesus had forgiven me of my sins, saving me from eternal damnation—would I receive this free gift today and invite him into my heart? I gratefully accepted this good news with each altar call. Hearing that I had received the good news, my youth-group brother declared to me, "Do you know the *only reason* the Lord doesn't snatch you up to heaven right this second to be with him is because he wants you to stay behind, here on earth, and take others with you?" This was the way the Christian story was told to me in the early days of my faith: This fallen world is without hope, but God is now rescuing people *out* of this world into heaven. My job, within that story, is to extend a free ticket of salvation to as many as I can before I go. That ticket will one day transport us to a different and glorious place—namely, the life-after-death heaven.

As I have ministered over the years, I have noticed similar themes in congregation members—assumptions that the gospel story is about (1) an *individualistic* faith that believes God is mostly concerned with the state of my soul, (2) an escapist, *otherworldly* faith that believes God has mostly given up on the world and is now rescuing people out of that world into heaven, and (3) a *private* faith that concerns itself with private devotion to God as believers wait to be taken away.

Yet as I kept reading my Bible, I realized that this was not the story Jesus seemed to tell throughout the Gospels! Here, we will examine a few of Jesus' key ministry moments to see what we may learn of how Jesus himself preached the gospel.

Jesus' Good News

The message proclaimed most persistently by our Lord Jesus was not "Repent and believe so that after you die, you will go to heaven" but "The time has *come*. The *kingdom* of God *has come near*" (Mark 1:15, emphasis added). The central message of the gospel is the upending proclamation of a new *king* and *king-dom* in the here and now, in a place where Caesars and Herods still believe themselves ultimate authorities. Jesus could have chosen different language to announce his gospel, like the language of family (which he does, on occasion), but instead, Jesus most consistently chooses the politically charged language of "kingdom" to announce his mission.

To say that Jesus' good news was "political" is not to claim that he waged a violent war against Rome or attempted to become emperor. Instead, as Obery Hendricks writes in *The Politics of Jesus*, the gospel Jesus announced "not only called for change in individual hearts but also demanded sweeping and comprehensive change in the political, social, and economic structures in his setting in life."[4] Additionally, the story of life-after-death salvation may still be true, but it is nowhere near the focus of Jesus' ministry on earth. Instead, Jesus ushers in the reign of God on earth today, with his resurrection operating as a sign to the world that new life is coming—not in an ethereal, cloud-filled realm, but here on the soil of this earth.[5]

Politics may refer to the coercive use of power employed by a state to maintain power and order, but it can also simply refer to *the way humans shape a common life together*. It is with this latter understanding of the word that we must recognize how inherently *political* the gospel of Jesus is. When we read the Gospels, we see that Jesus has a clear vision for what that common life together should be when it is ruled by a loving God who desires for all humans to flourish.

If politics is the way we structure our common life together as humans, what does a gospel politic look like?

The Lord's Prayer

Both versions of the Lord's Prayer (Matthew 6:9-13 and Luke 11:2-4) reveal a vision for the arrival of a Kingdom with new social, political, and economic realities that stood in stark contrast to Caesar's unjust empire.

Our Father in heaven. The prayer is directed to "our" Father. This is not a prayer for personal, individual needs. Those who follow Jesus are formed into a new social order framed not by hierarchy but by the reorganizing reality that God is *our* Father. In God's Kingdom, all are cared for because God is Father to all.

Hallowed be your Name. Your Kingdom come. Your will be done. Followers of Christ pray for the holiness of God's name to be made more manifest than any other, be it king, emperor, president, or political party. Hendricks explains the significance of this part of the prayer for early disciples: "Because Roman state religion required that Caesar's name alone be hallowed (one of Caesar's Greek titles was actually 'Soter,' or 'Savior'), this was a radical call."[6] Jesus teaches all his followers to pray that *God's* Kingdom—not Caesar's—come.

Give us this day our daily bread. And forgive us our debts. The economics of earthly kingdoms run on the principle of scarcity. There isn't enough bread for everyone—only for the privileged and powerful few. In this scarcity, debt is a method used to exploit the poor and powerless. Yet the Lord's Prayer defies the ruthless tools of commerce and empire in exchange for a new Kingdom economics. Hendricks writes:

This teaching on debt in particular might seem impractical in our complex world, but it has as much saliency today as it did in Jesus' time. Businesspersons can refuse to place profits before people. They can refuse to participate in unfair business dealings, refuse to pay substandard wages, refuse to force workers to labor without health-care or pension benefits, refuse to charge exorbitant interest rates and rental costs. For instance, Habitat for Humanity, a Christian organization that builds affordable housing for those in need, charges no interest on its mortgage loans. Its official Web site calls this "the economics of Jesus," which is described as "people act[ing] in response to human need, giving what they have without seeking profit or interest.[7]

The politics intrinsic to the Lord's Prayer direct us not to a private, individualized, otherworldly faith but to a faith that seeks to usher in and live out (1) an equitable social order where God is "Our Father"; (2) unswerving political allegiance to God and God's ways rather than to politicians, parties, and their methods; and (3) economic provision for all: "daily bread" and "release from debt" in a new world where people are prioritized above profit.

The Drama of the Sheep and the Goats

This well-known story tells of the Son of Man coming in glory at the end of time. As the nations gather before him, judgment is exercised. This drama is not describing a judgment of individuals but a collective judgment of nations. Nations are separated, as sheep are separated from goats, according to specific criteria. When we evaluate nations, we tend to do so on the basis of wealth, military power, and standard of living. But speaking in the tradition of the prophets who came before him, Jesus says the criteria he'll use for nations at the end of time will involve how well a nation cares for the poor, the sick, the immigrant, and the prisoner. Sacred care for the most unprotected in our world must shape our political imagination.

Jesus' Interaction with Political Persons and Places

The reality of Jesus' earthly existence was that from birth to death, Jesus lived as an oppressed subject in a territory ruled by Rome. Roman rule claimed to achieve peace for the inhabitants of its empire but brought pervasive suffering upon many. Jesus was no exception: He fled from King Herod's "Slaughter of the Innocents" as a young child, mourned the death of his relative John the Baptist at the careless decree of Herod Antipas, "suffered under Pontius Pilate" (as the Apostles' Creed says), and eventually died—at the hands of Rome—by an excruciating form of public execution used to invoke fear in the masses. Jesus did not choose the privilege of "staying out of politics." His life was written on the backdrop of a brutal regime that visibly affected every detail of his day, as well as the lives of those he loved.

As Jesus announced the coming of the Kingdom of God,

he also acted with purpose and intentionality toward the corrupt political forces of his day:

1. *Jesus refused to utilize coercion and violence when engaging political powers.* In the Sermon on the Mount, considered by some to be the essence of Jesus' political teaching, Jesus says: "Do not resist an evildoer" (Matthew 5:38-41, NRSV). Rather than arguing for *passive* resistance to evil (which Jesus' own actions would negate), this passage may better be understood as, "Do not *violently* resist an evildoer." Jesus knew his followers would face powerful opponents of the Kingdom of God, and he taught his disciples that they must learn how to, as Walter Wink eloquently phrases it, "[adopt] a way by which evil can be opposed without being mirrored, the oppressor resisted without being emulated, and the enemy neutralized without being destroyed."[8]

   When Jesus is arrested shortly before his trial and crucifixion, Peter draws his sword, cutting off one of the men's ears. Rather than commend Peter's use of force, Jesus says, "Put your sword back into its place; for all who take the sword will perish by the sword" (Matthew 26:52, NRSV). The Kingdom of God does not come through violence.

2. *Jesus exposed corruption and oppression.* While Jesus resisted using the tools of oppression, coercion, and

violence, he did strategically reveal and disrupt evil. All four of the New Testament Gospels include a narrative about Jesus visiting the Temple; driving out its merchants, traders, and animals; and effectively shutting down its business for the day. The Temple priests were powerful, selected and backed up by Rome for their allegiance, leaving them free to operate with greed and corruption.[9] Jesus directly confronts these powerful leaders in his clearing of the Temple because his Kingdom challenges their corruption.

Preach the Whole Gospel!

So preachers, pastors, and leaders of the church: Let us preach the gospel, indeed! Let us preach it in the manner that Jesus did—as the world-overturning announcement that right here, right now, God's Kingdom is entering our realm. This is one of the chief ways those in the pulpit can invite those in the pews into intentional discipleship. Preach the good news that announces the very political message that God's Kingdom of peace is coming, so that any current kingdom operating on violence and coercion is not part of the new world but part of the old order that is passing away (2 Corinthians 5:17). Preach the good news that God's Kingdom invites us into a new social, political, and economic order that no longer preserves wealth and power for the few but welcomes all to receive daily bread and release from debt. Preach the good news that Jesus is renewing humanity to care actively for one another, especially for the most vulnerable among us.

From the Pews: The Church's Call to Embody and Extend a Kingdom Politic

What does political discipleship look like for those in the pews of our churches? It may be preachers' work to begin the gospel proclamation in our communities, but it is our church communities who must *continue* that gospel proclamation by *embodying* and *extending* the politics of God's Kingdom in our families, neighborhoods, workplaces, and communities.

Embody

In my suburban town, there is an abundance of empty houses and vacant storefronts from a long season of financial downturn in our area. One of these smaller homes sat on a triangular lot at the busy intersection of three streets, more visible at this active crossroads. Each year, the grass and weeds grew taller, the windows more cracked, the roof slanted more steeply. Every season it sat uncared for, the sight became even more hopeless—a kind of symbol of what was happening to our whole town.

Finally, after eight or nine years of the property slowly decaying, a multigenerational Latino family moved there. Within months, they had renovated the house—piles of old floorboards stacked by the curb for pickup were signs of internal renewal. Outside, a large garden plot was plowed, with chicken wire around it to keep out critters. The grass was mowed, the weeds were chopped down. Eventually, patio lights were strung between the old trees that dot the property, two tire swings were hung from branches, and a barbecue grill emerged on the scene. Now, each weekend, all those driving by the busy intersection witness family and friends gathered over a bountiful meal, smoke pluming from the grill, and festive music playing. My heart is warmed each time I see this sight. It gives me hope for what may become of the other empty properties in our little town.

This is the kind of image the church is meant to be for the world—a sign of what is possible when a Kingdom of love and restoration comes. This is what Adam Gustine refers to in his book *Becoming a Just Church: Cultivating Communities of God's Shalom* as "the church as parable."[10] Parables are stories about ordinary subjects, like soil, seeds, and water, but they are a subversive force because far from simply depicting ordinary things, they also explain how the Kingdom of God works (and as we have seen, God's Kingdom works very differently than earthly kingdoms). In the same way, the church is to be ordinary yet subversive—a community where God's intentions for the world are already being lived out in an ordinary people. Historical theologian Justo González refers to the church as a *mañana* people—a people who live out God's vision for the future today.[11] Revelation 21:3 points to the day when God's Kingdom finally comes in full on earth: "Look! God's dwelling place is now among the people, and he will dwell with them. They will be his people, and God himself will be with them and be their God." That is the glorious *mañana* hope we have. Yet as the church, our task is to be this community today—ordering our common life, or our *politic*, according to God's Kingdom.[12]

Early Christians embodied a community whose social and economic life stood in stark contrast to the Roman Empire, and through their witness—not just their verbal or individual witness, but their witness as a collective people—they exposed the evil of Rome. The emperor Julian lamented that the Christians, whom he called Galileans, showed up Rome in their charitable care for people the empire deemed unworthy of resources, saying, "It is a disgrace that these impious Galileans care not only for their own poor, but for ours as well."[13] In the hospitality they showed toward the vulnerable and in their inclusion of the most marginalized, they were considered strange. Additionally, Kaitlyn Schiess writes:

> The apologist Tatian noted that the church included everyone in worship and organization, making "no distinctions in rank and outward appearance, or wealth and education, or age and sex." In a society where Roman men often pressured women to get dangerous abortions and let female infants die of exposure, the Christian community created lower mortality rates for women because of a different social ethic that valued the contributions of women—single and married—for the good of the community.[14]

The early church didn't just speak about a new Kingdom politic. They lived it in their concern for the sick and poor and in their refusal to kill their enemies. And they gave their ultimate love and allegiance to Christ as King, even at the expense of torture and death. Early Christians did not have voting rights (most election processes in Rome had been undermined by Caesar Augustus by Jesus' time, and even before that, only Roman male citizens could vote), nor could they politically lobby for their preferred policies.[15] But the early church had a political power that transcended those things—the power of their common life together, which bore witness to the truth that it is Jesus Christ, not Caesar, who is truly Lord.

Unfortunately, ask many people today and they will tell you that this is not the reputation that the church in the United States currently holds. It is the job of the church in the coming generations to reclaim its witness as an embodied "Kingdom of God" politic, so that we might become a "visible manifestation of God's deliverance breaking into our world in a tangible manner."[16] Much of this work must begin with repentance over the ways we are entangled in domination, greed, and inequity.

Extend

While the church will never be perfect in the living out of a Kingdom politic, committing ourselves to the distinct politic *internally* is imperative if we are to prophetically witness to the world and extend that politic into our neighborhoods, communities, and nations. As we do so, our love for neighbor and our call to care for the most vulnerable in our society will bring us into contact with the political machinations of our neighborhoods, villages, and nation. Pastor William H. Lamar IV says:

> We must be bold to advocate the politics of God's realm in the church and outside of the church. I tell political leaders that we can afford good education in Washington, D.C., because God requires it. I tell elected officials that we can pay a living wage because God requires it. I organize to put pressure on Democrats and Republicans because theirs is the politics of expediency, ours is the politics of a new heaven and a new earth.
>
> . . . Like Jesus, and many of my ancestors in faith, I want to live and to die for the politics of God's reign. If these politics do not animate our prayers, songs, sermons, and testimonies, our speech is reduced to sounding brass and tinkling cymbals.[17]

What does it look like for the church to extend the politics of the Kingdom with prophetic hope and to engage the political systems of our neighborhoods and nations? It must look like Jesus. An extended Kingdom politic looks like advocacy for the poor and unprotected. It looks like economic policies that alleviate the burden of debt, and social policies that honor all people as worthy of care and inclusion. It looks like an engagement out of love for our neighbors and communities, while maintaining a distinction in the *way* we are willing to accomplish our vision—not resorting to corruption, abuse of power, or violence, yet not shying away from exposing and naming these things when we see them.

The way of earthly politics is to ask, *What policies best serve me?* Yet disciples of Jesus must be formed out of the ways of a politic of self-interest into a politic of neighborly love.

Finally, while Republicans and Democrats in our nation's two-party system vie for our allegiance, as Christ followers we can recognize that either party will be greatly inadequate and undeserving of our full allegiance because no political party fully embodies the politics of Jesus. Given this reality, political diversity about US national politics will always exist within the church, and there will be vehement disagreements among the people in our pews about which candidate or which policy best embodies the politics of Jesus.

Faithful discipleship will engage in such disagreements as opportunities for deeper dialogue—and sincere challenge. In our differences, rather than seeking some middle ground or avoiding the messiness of disagreement altogether, we must let our commitment to the kind of politic named in this chapter be the basis for our unity, our guiding compass, and the grounds on which we challenge one another. Questions like, *What will this policy do for the most vulnerable populations among us?* or *How does this political strategy reflect the ways of Jesus?* must be part of the curriculum of our political discipleship and shared life.

IF MY PEOPLE HUMBLE THEMSELVES

Mandy Smith

I'VE COME TO THE END OF MYSELF.

Last week a prominent pastor took a partisan stance in a public forum. Two days later a different pastor wrote an op-ed to denounce the first pastor. Now Christians across the political spectrum are joining the fray in a public (and un-Christian) brawl. My friends with one foot out the church door are watching the debacle and edging further out. For them it's just more proof that Christians are toxic.

This month there's been much hubbub in my denomination as we prepare for next week's annual gathering. In recent months denominational leaders have come into conflict with a professor at one of the denomination's seminaries.

What began as theological debate is now taking on a political tenor as various congregations choose their allegiances. Conversations with colleagues are filled with dismay as we share stories of broken relationships and denominational disintegration.

And this week I'm navigating a much smaller, much closer conflict as I try to mop up a mess from last week's sermon. The passage seemed pretty straightforward to me, so I was surprised to receive several long, angry emails from people frustrated that I "got political." I'm trying to discern whether it's my job to dispel concerns or invite new imagination. And as I look over this week's sermon text, I'm anxious, wondering what land mines might be lurking in every passage I preach!

Perhaps a long email will fix all this mess? A meeting? A policy? A social-media post? There must be some way to overcome this personal, local, national, global, relational, theological, emotional, spiritual, existential crisis of the contemporary church.

But my clever email stays in draft mode. Nothing seems enough to calm the contention, to release us from these political strongholds. When it comes time to write my sermon, I huddle in my bed, wishing humans could hibernate. I can't calm my own fears, much less those of my congregants. Where is God in this mess? Why has he given us an impossible task?

Things are crumbling around our ears. We can see the ways the church is entangled with the world's ways. We're pained by how we've done Kingdom things in empire ways, how we've defined ourselves by national identity rather than by our identity in Christ.

This sense that something is wrong leads us to analyze, critique, and problem solve. Our assessment might sound like this: We need new approaches and restored energies to save our witness to a watching world. We need to learn how to have civilized conversations again. We need to undo the damage done by Christians who sound more like political extremists than Jesus. We need to fix this now, for God's sake. And until we do, our mission is defunct. (And in the meantime, every polarizing argument between Christians who claim to worship the same Lord, every denomination that splits over political differences, every sermon which sounds more like tribalism than the gospel affirms our fear that we're far from hope.)

There's no doubt that the contemporary Western church is in a serious state. Sadly, our history tells one story after another of cultural compromise, empire enmeshment, and power abuse. We see how much we go to extremes, either retreating from culture or losing ourselves in it. We've compromised our uniqueness, tarnished our witness. It's a desperate situation.

In this desperate, seemingly hopeless situation we have a choice—to continue in the old empire ways of fixing, controlling, understanding in our own power, or to do something that upends empire. If we're not careful, we'll just keep the same anxious, self-sufficient spirit and put it in a new box. And when those efforts come up empty, we'll be tempted to just despair. If we're not careful, in all our efforts to fix our enmeshment with the ways of the world, we'll persist in the world's ways of "fixing" things (which always lead to violence of one kind or another). We'll miss the invitation to be made new. In our desire for external, systemic change, we miss the opportunity to be changed. The best way to stop doing Kingdom things in empire ways is to allow ourselves to be transformed by the Kingdom. And the Kingdom will not stop until we're made like Christ.

If we steward our desperation well, the desperation itself may, surprisingly, be the door to hope. To engage this opportunity, we'll need to open our hearts to reimagine what it even is we're hoping for. If we assume that this desperate situation will only be fixed when we've redesigned all our institutions and healed all the ways church has enmeshed with culture, a solution is a long way off. But there's an even better solution available to us right now—at the same time easier and harder, more available and more transformative than all the things we've been working so hard to do.

The Kingdom solution is to let our desperation become a cry for help, simply confessing our need for God. That turning of our heart is, in itself, the answer. Of course, it won't change the external realities—the structures of the world or of our broken church. The conflicts, the unhealthy systems, the unsatisfying habits, will all remain when we open our eyes from that prayer of turning. Which will be very unsatisfying to our empire habit of measuring outcomes. But this turning of our hearts will change us—one heart, one congregation at a time—reminding us where our true hope lies. A release will take place in us which will allow us to see everything—ourselves, the church, the world, our nation and leaders, our mission—in a new way. In an instant, in the falling of a tear, in the bending of a knee, we will be released to discover that the answer is right here within us, if we'll just stop striving in our own power long enough to reconnect with a different Power.

◆　　◆　　◆

As I came to the end of this exhausting week, not much had changed. The toxic public debate between prominent pastors, the denominational divisions, the stepping around land mines in my own congregation all remained. I had put together something of a sermon, but it felt lifeless. As did I. God seemed to have left me out on a limb, and I began the Sunday service feeling numb. The heartfelt worship of others judged my frosty heart. The reverent readings of Scripture spoke from far away. I repeated my demands: *Have you forgotten your church? Where is your provision? Why have you given us this impossible situation? Answer for yourself!*

But one song disarmed me, drew tears from my anger. I fought the lyrics stirring my heart: "Alleluia. . . . Worthy is the Lamb. . . . You are holy."[1] If I could have shaped my mouth into sincere words, it would have sounded more like, "Are you even watching the state of things? Do you still care?" I certainly didn't feel like telling God how worthy or holy he is. But although I didn't *feel* like worshiping God, I *needed* to worship God. Not because God demands I cower and defer to boost his ego. But because this is truth: He *is* worthy. He *is* holy.

Thankfully, God has space for his children to honestly express their frustration. The Psalms give us permission to demand, "Are you even listening?!" And once we've beaten our small fists on his chest long enough, our demands turn into sobs and we can finally release into him. We can release into the truth of who he is—not for the sake of his ego but for our own sakes. The Truth will set us free. And the Truth is: He will not change to conform to our small imaginations of who we are or who he is. The Truth is: we are healed when we acknowledge who he *actually* is. As much as we think our problems can only be resolved when God defends his actions and acquiesces to our demands, he knows something better. And he is big enough to be in the mess with us until we figure that out, over and over. In fact, he longs for the intimacy that grows in the mess.

As we navigate cultural Christianity, living in both empire and Kingdom, we find ourselves in a contentious place. Much damage has been done, and much is yet to be healed. The empire drives us: work, strive, fret, fix, control, understand. Will you break that empire cycle? Will you release your desperation into the One who does not despair? It may not seem like much to just change one human heart, but it's all any one of us has the power to do. Any effort to force this change on others just becomes more power abuse.

In 2 Chronicles 7:14-16 God says:

If my people, who are called by my name, will
humble themselves and pray and seek my face and
turn from their wicked ways, then I will hear from
heaven, and I will forgive their sin and will heal
their land. Now my eyes will be open and my ears
attentive to the prayers offered in this place. I have
chosen and consecrated this temple so that my
Name may be there forever. My eyes and my heart
will always be there.

Passages like this make God sound temperamental, even
coercive: "Unless you do things my way, I'm withdrawing
my blessings." God seems like a manipulative parent: "Until
you obey, I'm not giving you dinner." We imagine a transac-
tion: I do *x* for God, and God does *y* for me. And the things
that keep God happy can feel random and unreasonable. Is
he testing us, seeing if we'll check items off his odd list of
favorite things? It becomes a two-step process—

1. Do random thing that God wants.
2. Be back in relationship with God.

But the things God actually wants always have a direct
correlation to restored relationship. Humbling ourselves has
the natural outcome of reconnection. Softening our hearts
leads to relationship. Confessing our underestimation of

him leads to reunion. Repenting of our prideful independence leads to communion once more.

We may not have consciously walked away from God or chosen to depend on human leaders and systems rather than God. In fact, it often feels like *we* went nowhere, that *God* is the one who moved away from *us*. So it's only right to feel entitled, bruised by the distance. *Where did you go, God? Why aren't you bringing the kind of justice you taught us to long for? Why haven't you transformed our nation?* But these questions rarely get an answer. God is not in the business of defending himself.

In 2 Chronicles 7 God calls people to turn from their wicked ways so he can forgive their sin. But we didn't lie, cheat, steal, lust. While there are certainly many stories of moral failure in the contemporary church, most of our mission isn't failing because of obvious sin. Most of our public expressions of faith are well-meaning. Yet, we've enmeshed with the empires of our time, engaging in unhealthy ways with the world's politics, economics, values, methods. And even in our reckoning with that, as we fix the errors of our history, we perpetuate our deeper, heart-level sin: Like Abraham turning to Hagar, we've taken things into our own hands (Genesis 16).

Like Abraham, we've committed the sin of thinking our plans are wiser than God's, our imagination is bigger, our timing is better, our agency is more powerful. We've taken on the habits of our secular culture, which drive us to fix, control, understand in our own strength. We've forgotten that we belong in him, beyond national identity, beyond political agendas. We've forgotten that he makes all things new and that his Spirit is still at work through his church, small and insignificant though it may seem compared to the vastness of the empire around it.

I've been in many conversations about the desperate situation of the church, critiquing old ways and brainstorming new. Often I've left even more discouraged and exhausted, with thoughts like these: *So much work to heal all the division, cast vision beyond tribalism, model conversations of peace in a climate of anxiety. Will we ever see that healing in our lifetimes? We have so much baggage to overcome, so many missteps to heal. We're just trying to do the things God asks us to do! Why hasn't he fixed his broken church yet?*

Instead of gathering more statistics and trying to problem solve, what might it mean for us to shape spaces for lament, where together we turn to God in our pain and despair, confessing our tiredness and brokenness and learning once more to need him? It might require us, as brothers and sisters, to let down our guards with one another and with God, to name our own collusion, and to cry out. We'll still leave with tears and tiredness, but we'll also leave with new hope. We are no longer alone. We may not have the solutions we thought we needed, but we have something better—an expanded imagination that the One who holds the universe is not despairing. The One who makes all things new is still making things new. God has gone nowhere. In that humbling place, we have an opportunity not only to talk about God's sovereignty but to practice our belief in it, to turn to him as if his reign is unshaken, even in the midst of upheaval. After entering that space, we return to the world with new vision. Humbling ourselves and seeking God's face allows us to be connected once more to the source of all we need.

Empire is interested only in things that look like life—strong, finished, uncomplicated things. But such is not the nature of our actual limited, unfinished, messy human existence. Empire tells us that emptying will leave us with nothing, that lament is a loss of control which we can never regain. But empire knows nothing of our three-part journey: Life, Death, Resurrection (which Richard Rohr calls Order, Disorder, Reorder).[2] It's the only way transformation happens. As much as empire likes the idea of transformation, it will keep us forever in the current order because it lacks the stomach for disorder and the imagination for what emerges from it.

A Liturgy of Emptying in Desperation

Liturgy literally means "work of the people."[3] Use the following liturgy to guide you and your faith community or small group in the work of releasing empire and emptying to God.

◆　◆　◆

Create a space (for prayer, silence, journaling) for participants to reflect on what is wrong in ourselves, the world, the church.

Participants may share from that reflection in a phrase or sentence (spoken aloud or written on a board).

Together, read Psalm 13:1-2:

> How long, LORD? Will you forget me forever?
>   How long will you hide your face from me?
> How long must I wrestle with my thoughts
>   and day after day have sorrow in my heart?
>   How long will my enemy triumph over me?

Provide a few moments of silence and invite participants to speak a sentence prayer in response to the psalm.

Create a space (for prayer, silence, journaling) for participants to reflect on how they feel about the current state of society.

Invite participants to share from that reflection in a phrase or sentence (spoken aloud or written on a board).

Together, read Psalm 13:3-4:

> Look on me and answer, LORD my God.
>   Give light to my eyes, or I will sleep in death,
> and my enemy will say, "I have overcome him,"
>   and my foes will rejoice when I fall.

Silence is kept. Participants may speak a sentence prayer in response to the psalm.

Create a space (for prayer, silence, journaling) for participants to reflect on who God is in this broken situation (even if we can't see or feel him).

Participants may share from that reflection in a phrase or sentence (spoken aloud or written on a board).

Together, read Psalm 13:5-6:

> But I trust in your unfailing love;
>   my heart rejoices in your salvation.
> I will sing the LORD's praise,
>   for he has been good to me.

Silence is kept. Participants may speak a prayer in response to the psalm.

Confession:

> *We confess that we are not all-powerful.*
> *Our understanding is not enough.*
> *Our power is not enough.*
> *We have relied on other powers.*
> *We confess we need you, Lord.*

We confess we are not powerless.
You have given us voices.
You have given us resources and agency.
We confess we have neglected and misused them.
We give them to you for your service, Lord.
Amen.

Take Communion together.

Close with prayer:

In Jesus' body, you told us a story of life, death, resurrection.
Thank you that you are no stranger to brokenness and
 disorder.
Thank you for your imagination beyond all that seems like
 death to us.
We want to trust that you are still making all things new.
Show us how to join you in your messy, marvelous work.
Give us your imagination.
Give us your hope.
We need you.
Amen.

❖   ❖   ❖

This humility God desires is not groveling or self-loathing.
Humility is knowing that he is God and we are not. Humility
is knowing that we need something beyond our small selves.
When we do our part—humble ourselves—God is able to

do his part—hear. Second Chronicles 7 is not a checklist for us (humble ourselves, pray, seek God's face) but an unpacking of what it means to humble—a humble heart naturally pursues God, turning from its own self-sufficient ways. And neither is it a checklist of things God does but a vision of how he hears our humility—with forgiveness and healing.

God is not that parent, wheedling, "Until you obey, I'm not giving you dinner." A humble posture allows us to instead hear him saying, "Unless you trust that I provide good food and choose to open your mouth, I can't feed you. Don't be surprised that you're starving if you won't receive what I offer." Here's where our God is very unlike a tyrant who demands sycophantic surrender: He will not force us. Like any good parent, he very clearly describes the consequences of our choices, and he lets us experience them. Not to harm us but so we can learn once more that he is our home. Every exile is an invitation.

Children who never experience consequences become malformed, stunted in their awareness of their own agency. God's invitation to humble ourselves, pray and seek his face, is an invitation to embrace our agency. He says: I have not moved from you. ("My eyes and my heart will always be there"; 2 Chronicles 7:16.) He waits for us to use that agency again, to turn toward him. As much as he longs for it (for his sake and for ours), he won't force it. Will we set aside our desperate, independent efforts at accomplishing God's goals without God's help?

A PRAYER OF TURNING BACK TO GOD

Where your church has lost its way, we cry, "Abba, Father!"
Where human life is cheap, we cry, "Abba, Father!"
Where we consume one another, we cry, "Abba, Father!"
Where we see with eyes of mistrust and hate, we cry,
    "Abba, Father!"
Where families are torn apart, we cry, "Abba, Father!"
Where cities are in distress, we cry, "Abba, Father!"
Where the powerful abuse the needy, we cry, "Abba,
    Father!"
Where food is withheld from the hungry, we cry, "Abba,
    Father!"
Where we have destroyed the beauty of your creation, we
    cry, "Abba, Father!"
In every way we are small, afraid, broken, alone, and
    desperate, we cry, "Abba, Father!"
In the face of a spirit of slavery and fear, we cry, "Abba,
    Father!"
Let your Spirit testify to our spirits that we are your
    children.
Amen.

◆　◆　◆

God himself is hidden in every longing of our hearts. His heart remains open, always waiting for us to turn and rest in him again. What he offers us is risky and personal—not a contract but intimacy. He longs to call us by his name once more, to hear and forgive and heal once more. As he promises in 2 Chronicles 7, his eyes are always open, his ears always attentive, his heart always available. When we choose to set aside our habits of self-sufficiency and turn back to God, we are home.

Our nation might be in crisis, our world might be torn by war, our neighborhoods might be crying for justice. When we reconnect, over and over, with this God who has gone nowhere, we're reminded of the truth—that he cares more about the crisis, the war, the injustice than we do. We can look in the timeless, unchanging, ever-new face of God, whose reign has outlived the empires of Babylon, Egypt, and Rome and who watches the rise and fall of every earthly power. We reconnect with his perspective—he has not given up. He calls us to embody his peace and justice, dependent not on human powers and political structures but on his ever-present Spirit.

When we live in humble connection to God as the source of all hope, power, and belonging, we have what we need to bring something new to the world. When we—over and over—refuse to put our hope in human powers, we have an unquenchable source of a different kind of hope, one not unsettled by human empires rising and falling. Because we know a Kingdom that grows like yeast, infusing everything, unseen. Hard to see, harder to measure, but also harder to overcome, drawing us into God's slow, messy, wonderful work of making all things new.

A New Pledge of Citizenship

Let us now declare this hope through this oath to the Kingdom of God:

> I hereby declare that I absolutely renounce all allegiance to any human prince, potentate, state, or sovereignty of which I have been a subject or citizen; that I will seek the Kingdom of God above all else; that I will proclaim that Kingdom even when I can't see it.

> I declare that I will lay down my rights to the will of God, pursuing the good of the Kingdom above my own preferences, trusting that this life is also for my good.

> I will serve the way of the Kingdom wherever I go, with my energies, resources, and gifts, trusting that God will equip me with all I need to follow his call.

> I promise—even when obedience leads to suffering— to find solidarity in Jesus, remembering both his sacrifice and his resurrection.

> I make a covenant to guard my imagination for abundance in scarcity, for strength in what feels like weakness, for victory in what feels like defeat.

I acknowledge my need for God's help even to live out these promises.

I pledge allegiance to Jesus (who has pledged allegiance to me), trusting that everything I lose he has lost, that everything he has gained I also gain.

Amen.[4]

CONTINUING THE CONVERSATION
Questions for Reflection and Discussion

KINGDOM CONVERSATIONS raise the stakes, as we allow God to bring his higher thoughts to bear on our limited vision and finite wisdom. We don't just interact thoughtfully; we do so prayerfully, subjecting ourselves to the sovereignty of a God who loves us and wants good for us and from us. And we do so both individually and collectively, not settling merely for personal reflection that deepens our private piety, or for dialogue that ends in chin-stroking self-congratulation. Rather, we engage in honest and humble conversation with God, with ourselves, and with others so we can see where Jesus is leading us now to proclaim and demonstrate, near and far, that God is here, God is good, and God is for us. A Kingdom conversation has the potential, in small and big ways, to transform the world.

What follows are questions to prime the pump for a Kingdom conversation about national identity and faithfulness to God. Almost every question is designed to be considered from two perspectives: personally, for the purposes of private and public reflection and confession; and corporately, in order to listen to and learn from other perspectives, to learn to love one another, and to seek God together as a faith community.

The questions are organized by chapter in case you wish to move slowly through the book together. If you wish to discuss the book as a whole in one conversation, it's best to review the questions ahead of time and focus together on the questions that help you move from curiosity to conviction, from head to heart to hands.

Introduction

- Why did you decide to read this book?
- What are you hoping—or concerned—that this book might say, or might not say?

Chapter 1: Can We Have a Conversation?

- Have you ever experienced the type of tension that is described about the Brownlee Home Group? What did it feel like for you?
- What response is most common for you in political conversations? Do you feel the need to convince others of your opinions? Do you feel anger or angst? Do you feel triggered?
- What are the roots of your responses? Are you aware of the effects of your own story? Are your responses rooted in opinion or in fact?

- How can you better facilitate open, safe conversations in your own relationships?

Chapter 2: The Kingdom of God Is Here

- If someone were to ask you to describe the Kingdom of God, what would you say?
- In what ways is the reality of God's Kingdom a comfort to you? In what ways is it a challenge?
- Is Christ the undisputed King of your life? If not, what areas of your life might need to be rearranged to place them under his loving authority?
- What are some ways you can bring the Kingdom near and join God's work in the world by planting "mustard seeds" in your own neighborhood?

Chapter 3: A History of Kingdoms in Conflict

- Compared to the historical descriptions in this chapter, would you say that Christians in your own country and context today are suspicious outsiders, energetic upstarts, privileged insiders, or persecuted enemies? How do you think *others* in your country view Christians?
- What are the gods of your surrounding culture, and how do you and your faith community refuse to bow down to these gods?
- What are the potential opportunities and dangers associated with seeking and using power within human political systems to enact moral or spiritual change?

- How do you think our current political climate and events will be interpreted theologically by generations to come?

Chapter 4: Under the Authority of Another

- When you feel you are suffering, how easy or difficult is it for you to trust God, his perspective, and his plan?
- In Matthew 10:16, Jesus instructs his disciples to be "as shrewd as snakes and as innocent as doves." When Christians are outsiders in a country or culture, how can we know when and how to be subversive?
- Would outside observers view your church or faith community as being Spirit-led? What are the fruits and marks of your community that have been shaped by the Spirit?
- What "imperial noise" have you allowed to shape you? What are specific, practical ways you can tune out this noise and focus instead on "local tradition" such as prayer, Scripture, worship, and other Spirit-led practices?

Chapter 5: The Ethics of Allegiance

- How do you feel about the Pledge of Allegiance to the American flag (or similar expressions of loyalty in your country)? Have you stopped to consider the words? Does it bother you when someone acts in a way you feel is disrespectful to your flag or to the country "for which it stands"?

- In all honesty, what or whom has your true allegiance? What would your words and actions tell someone else about what takes priority in your life?
- Are there times when your religion or your country have gotten in the way of loving your neighbor? When and how?
- What needs to be reordered in your life to pledge your full allegiance to Christ?

Chapter 6: Nation as Narrative

- What narrative do you hold regarding your nation? Who and what has shaped your understanding?
- What parts of this narrative are rooted in truth, and what is untrue or mythical? What has been the impact of this narrative on your attitudes and behaviors toward others?
- How do you honestly feel about the author's idea that the United States "has never been (nor ever will be) a wholly Christian nation?" Do you agree or disagree? Why?
- Who is someone around you who might have a different narrative from yours? Have you asked them about their perspective? If not, how might you open a conversation with them? How might you make space in your own national narrative for those with other narratives?

Chapter 7: Strangers in a Strange Land

- Have you ever been in another country or other environment where you were a stranger or outsider? Describe the situation and what the experience was like.
- Have you fully embraced your status as a spiritual "stranger" in this world, a person whose primary citizenship is with heaven, not on earth? Which temptation is stronger for you—disengagement or dominion?
- How can you help translate the message of the gospel to the people among whom you are a Kingdom sojourner?
- How can you more regularly practice hospitality toward others, welcoming them as true Kingdom brothers and sisters?

Chapter 8: My Fellow Citizens

- Where have you seen the "New Samaria" emerging in your country and in your own community?
- Reflect on the idea of "unity in the midst of diversity." What might this look like in your faith community? What are some of the challenges of this concept?
- What are your own personal biases that may blind you to seeing what God sees? (You might ask a trusted friend to help you identify them.)
- What are the walls—either physical or virtual—that separate people in your part of the world? What can you do to help break down these walls? What "right,

might, or fright" might you need to give up to work toward unity?

Chapter 9: Politics, Pulpit, and Pew

- Before reading this chapter, what was your definition of, view of, and involvement in "politics"?
- What kind of "politics" does your church or faith community preach and practice? How are these politics lived out?
- What is your *mañana* vision for a gospel politic, and what are specific ways you can make that hope and future a reality today in your own city or community?
- How might you or your faith community need to repent for ways you have been entangled in the politics of greed, dominion, or inequity?

Chapter 10: If My People Humble Themselves

- What do you feel when you think about your country—both its current state and its future? Do you find yourself anxious, angry, desperate, hopeful? What causes these feelings for you?
- When is the last time you repented or lamented regarding your country's brokenness and your contribution to it? When is the next time you will do so?
- Slowly read "A Prayer of Turning Back to God," reflecting on each word. Where do you long for healing in your life?

- Slowly read "A New Pledge of Citizenship." Can you say that this is truly your desire, your pledge, your plan? What is one specific way you can live out this pledge in the next week?

NOTES

CHAPTER 1: CAN WE HAVE A CONVERSATION?

1. Eugene H. Peterson, *The Jesus Way: A Conversation on the Ways that Jesus Is the Way* (Grand Rapids, MI: Eerdmans, 2007), 4.
2. Online Etymology Dictionary, s.v. "controversial (*adj.*)," accessed December 8, 2021, https://www.etymonline.com/word/controversial #etymonline_v_28807.
3. Online Etymology Dictionary, s.v. "contentious (*adj.*)," accessed November 10, 2021, https://www.etymonline.com/word/contentious.
4. See David W. Angel, "The Four Types of Conversations: Debate, Dialogue, Discourse, and Diatribe," Medium.com, December 31, 2016, https://medium.com/@DavidWAngel/the-four-types-of-conversations -debate-dialogue-discourse-and-diatribe-898d19eccc0a.
5. W. Gerrod Parrott, ed., *Emotions in Social Psychology: Essential Readings* (Philadelphia: Psychology Press, 2001), 36.
6. Regarding children, see Matthew 18:1-6; regarding lepers, see Mark 1:41; regarding Samaritans, see Luke 10:33-37.
7. For further reading on anger, see Glenn Taylor and Rod Wilson, *Exploring Your Anger: Friend or Foe?* (Grand Rapids, MI: Baker Books, 1997).
8. Anna Wierzbicka, "Angst," *Culture and Psychology* 4, no. 2 (June 1998): 161–188.
9. For further reflection, see Junchol Park et al., "Anxiety Evokes Hypofrontality and Disrupts Rule-Relevant Encoding by Dorsomedial Prefrontal Cortex Neurons," *Journal of Neuroscience* 36, no. 11 (March 2016): 3322–35; and Michael J. Mannor et al., "Heavy Lies the Crown?

How Job Anxiety Affects Top Executive Decision Making in Gain and Loss Contexts," *Strategic Management Journal* 37, no. 9 (September 2016): 1968–89.

10. Frank Amthor, *Neuroscience for Dummies*, 2nd ed. (Hoboken, NJ: Wiley, 2016), 45–46. See also Mia Belle Frothingham, "Fight, Flight, Freeze, or Fawn: What This Response Means," SimplyPsychology, October 6, 2021, https://www.simplypsychology.org/fight-flight-freeze-fawn.html.

CHAPTER 2: THE KINGDOM OF GOD IS HERE

1. Dallas Willard, *The Divine Conspiracy: Rediscovering Our Hidden Life in God* (San Francisco: HarperSanFrancisco, 1998), chap. 2.

2. Scot McKnight, *One.Life: Jesus Calls, We Follow* (Grand Rapids, MI: Zondervan, 2010), 16–17.

3. Ronald Sider, "What if We Defined the Gospel the Way Jesus Did?" in Brian Woolnough and Wonsuk Ma, eds., *Holistic Mission: God's Plan for God's People*, Regnum Edinburgh 2010 Series (Cornwall, UK: Regnum, 2010), 17, http://digitalshowcase.oru.edu/re2010series/4.

4. See also 2 Samuel 6:2; 1 Kings 19:15; 1 Chronicles 13:6; 16:31; Psalms 22:3; 33:14; 55:19; 80:1; 99:1; 102:12; 123:1; Isaiah 33:22; 37:16.

5. Ben Witherington III, *Imminent Domain: The Story of the Kingdom of God and Its Celebration* (Grand Rapids, MI: Eerdmans, 2009), 4.

6. 1 Chronicles 16:33-34; Psalms 23:5; 36:8; 78:25; 105:40; Isaiah 2:4; 11:6-7; 52:7; Jeremiah 40:12; Micah 4:4. "With a dance in their heads" is a reference to the popular nineteenth-century Christmas poem "A Visit from St. Nicholas": "The children were nestled all snug in their beds; / While visions of sugar-plums danced in their heads."

7. See also Luke 9:2, 60; 10:8-9, 11.

8. Lesslie Newbigin, "Mission in Christ's Way: Bible Studies," Newbigin.net, accessed December 8, 2021, https://newbiginresources.org/wep-content /uploads/2016/12/87mcw.pdf: "We are still defining God and God's rule on the basis of something other than what is given in the total fact of Jesus—his life, ministry, death and resurrection. And when we do that, we end up not with a gospel, but with an ideology, a programme."

9. Mark Lau Branson and Alan J. Roxburgh, *Leadership, God's Agency, and Disruptions: Confronting Modernity's Wager* (Eugene, OR: Cascade Books, 2021).

10. Witherington, *Imminent Domain*, 5–6.

11. A food forest is a self-sustaining (as all forests through the centuries are) edible ecosystem with seven layers from underground to canopy—for example, from onions and leeks to strawberries, to asparagus and rhubarb

to shrub berries, to apple, pear, and plum trees. We received a grant as a neighborhood, which helped us get started using permaculture and neighborhood "muscle." We're already enjoying not only its delicious produce but also the community connections and environmental benefits (e.g., the bees and butterflies love our flowers too!).

CHAPTER 3: A HISTORY OF KINGDOMS IN CONFLICT

1. Tertullian, Apology 40.2, in *Apology: De Spectaculis*, trans. T. R. Glover, Loeb Classical Library (Cambridge, MA: Harvard University Press, 1978).
2. Eusebius, *Life of Constantine* Book III, chap. 15 (NPNF 2/01:524).
3. Robert Louis Wilken, *The Christians as the Romans Saw Them*, 2nd ed. (New Haven, CT: Yale University Press, 2003), xviii, xix.
4. Tacitus, *Annals* 15.44.2–5, quoted in Larry W. Hurtado, *Destroyer of the gods: Early Christian Distinctiveness in the Roman World* (Waco, TX: Baylor University Press, 2016), 21.
5. On these themes see Hurtado, *Destroyer of the gods*, chap. 5, and David M. Scholer, ed., *Social Distinctives of the Christians in the First Century: Pivotal Essays by E. A. Judge* (Peabody, MA: Hendrickson, 2008), chap. 1.
6. Quoted in Philip Jenkins, *The Lost History of Christianity: The Thousand-Year Golden Age of the Church in the Middle East, Africa, and Asia—and How It Died* (New York: HarperCollins, 2008), 55–56.
7. Elizabeth Isichei, *A History of Christianity in Africa: From Antiquity to the Present* (Grand Rapids, MI: Eerdmans, 1995), 32.
8. Philip R. Amidon, trans., *The Church History of Rufinus of Aquileia*, Books 10 and 11 (Oxford: Oxford University Press, 1997), 10.9.19.
9. Amidon, *Church History*, 10.9.19.
10. Isichei, *History of Christianity in Africa*, 33.
11. David Bentley Hart, *The Story of Christianity: A History of 2,000 Years of the Christian Faith* (New York: Quercus, 2015), 84–85.
12. The term is Robert Louis Wilken's. See *The First Thousand Years: A Global History of Christianity* (New Haven, CT: Yale University Press, 2012), 216–17.
13. George Blaurock, "Reminiscences of George Blaurock," in *Spiritual and Anabaptist Writers: Documents Illustrative of the Radical Reformation*, ed. George H. Williams (Philadelphia: Westminster, 1957), 45–46.
14. Carter Lindberg, *The European Reformations* (Malden, MA: Blackwell, 1996), 215.
15. Bruce Gordon, *Calvin* (New Haven, CT: Yale University Press, 2009), 232.
16. Martin Luther, "Temporal Authority: To What Extent It Should Be

Obeyed," quoted in Timothy F. Lull, ed., *Martin Luther's Basic Theological Writings* (Minneapolis: Fortress, 1989), 688.

17. Quoted in Lull, *Martin Luther's Basic Theological Writings*, 689.

18. Paul Althaus, *Die deutsche Stunde der Kirche* (Göttingen: Vandenhoeck & Ruprecht, 1934), 5. Translation mine.

19. On this theme, see Richard Steigmann-Gall, *The Holy Reich: Nazi Conceptions of Christianity, 1919–1945* (Cambridge: Cambridge University Press, 2003); and Robert P. Ericksen, *Theologians Under Hitler: Gerhard Kittel, Paul Althaus, Emanuel Hirsch* (New Haven, CT: Yale University Press, 1985).

20. See Susannah Heschel, *The Aryan Jesus: Christian Theologians and the Bible in Nazi Germany* (Princeton, NJ: Princeton University Press, 2008), especially chap. 2.

21. Paul Althaus, *Der Trost Gottes: Predigten in schwerer Zeit* (Gütersloh: Bertelsmann, 1946), 246. Translation mine.

22. Barmen Declaration, articles II.1 and II.3, cited in Arthur C. Cochrane, *The Church's Confession Under Hitler*, 2nd ed. (Eugene, OR: Pickwick, 1976), 239, 241.

CHAPTER 4: UNDER THE AUTHORITY OF ANOTHER

1. Emphasis added.

2. Translation comes from *The Book of Common Prayer* (New York: Oxford University Press, 2008), 761.

3. John Goldingay, *Theological Diversity and the Authority of the Old Testament* (Grand Rapids, MI: Eerdmans, 1987), 65.

4. Walter Brueggemann, *Out of Babylon* (Nashville: Abingdon, 2010), 18.

5. Brueggemann, *Out of Babylon*, 84.

6. Brueggemann, *Out of Babylon*, 90–91.

7. N. T. Wright, "The New Testament and the 'State,'" *Themelios* 16, no. 1 (October/November 1990), 14.

8. N. T. Wright and Michael F. Bird, *The New Testament in Its World: An Introduction to the History, Literature, and Theology of the First Christians* (Grand Rapids, MI: Zondervan Academic, 2019), 94.

9. Various would-be Galilean messiahs like Simon of Peraea, Athronges the Shepherd, and Judas the Galilean had led revolts in the years before Jesus began his public ministry. They understood their revolts as Kingdom-of-God movements, using violent means to restore the kingdom to Israel in response to what they perceived as provocation from the Roman Empire. See N. T. Wright, *The New Testament and the People of God* (Minneapolis: Fortress, 1989), 172–173.

10. C. E. B. Cranfield, *Romans: A Shorter Commentary* (Grand Rapids, MI: Eerdmans, 1985), 321.

11. Dr. King is quoting Augustine with these words. See Martin Luther King Jr., "Letter from a Birmingham Jail," in *A Testament of Hope: The Essential Writings and Speeches of Martin Luther King Jr.*, ed. James Melvin Washington (New York: HarperCollins, 1986), 293.

CHAPTER 5: THE ETHICS OF ALLEGIANCE

1. By "national liturgies" I mean performative acts we engage in corporately like reciting the Pledge of Allegiance and standing for the national anthem.

2. Matthew W. Bates, *Salvation by Allegiance Alone: Rethinking Faith, Works, and the Gospel of Jesus the King* (Grand Rapids, MI: Baker Academic, 2017), 5.

3. Moral emotion ethics involves a variety of social emotions which inform decision-making. For more on moral emotion ethics, see https://www.ncbi.nlm.nih.gov/pmc/articles/PMC3083636/.

4. See Augustine, *City of God*, XV.23.

5. Michael Frost, "Colin Kaepernick vs. Tim Tebow: A Tale of Two Christians on Their Knees," *Washington Post*, September 24, 2017, https://www.washingtonpost.com/news/acts-of-faith/wp/2017/09 /24/colin-kaepernick-vs-tim-tebow-a-tale-of-two-christianities-on -its-knees/.

6. Antoine de Saint-Exupéry, quoted in James K. A. Smith, *You Are What You Love: The Spiritual Power of Habit* (Grand Rapids, MI: Brazos, 2016), 11.

7. Barbara Brown Taylor, *Holy Envy: Finding God in the Faith of Others* (New York: HarperOne, 2020), 208.

8. Shira Schoenberg, "Jewish Prayers: The Shema," Jewish Virtual Library, accessed November 8, 2021, https://www.jewishvirtuallibrary.org/the -shema.

9. Martin Luther King Jr., "I Have a Dream," speech, August 28, 1963, Washington, DC.

CHAPTER 6: NATION AS NARRATIVE

1. Lecrae, "Welcome to America," *Anomaly* © 2014 Reach Records.

2. "Welcome to America by Lecrae," Songfacts, accessed August 16, 2021, https://www.songfacts.com/facts/lecrae/welcome-to-america.

3. For more on George Bancroft, see Colin Woodard, "The Pitfalls and Promise of America's Founding Myths," *Smithsonian Magazine*,

February 22, 2021, https://www.smithsonianmag.com/history /determining-americas-national-myth-will-determine-countrys-fate -180977067/.

4. David Brooks, "The Four American Narratives," *New York Times*, May 26, 2017, https://www.nytimes.com/2017/05/26/opinion/the-four -american-narratives.html.

5. Arnold Friberg, *The Prayer at Valley Forge*, 1975, painting; "The U.S. Constitution (Full Text)," Interactive Constitution (by National Constitution Center), accessed December 3, 2021, constitutioncenter .org/interactive-constitution/full-text; "Benjamin Franklin, August 20, 1776, Proposal for United States Seal," Library of Congress, accessed December 3, 2021, https://www.loc.gov/item/mtjbib000186/.

6. This phrase is taken from Lukas Kwong, "An Open Letter on Anti-Asian Racism & Christian Nationalism," January 2021, https://www .againstchristianxenophobia.com/read-sign/i-why-were-speaking-up.

7. "'I've Been to the Mountaintop,' by Dr. Martin Luther King, Jr.," AFSCME, accessed November 8, 2021, https://www.afscme.org /about/history/mlk/mountaintop.

8. Cara Bentley, "Biden Quotes Isaiah, 'Here I Am Lord, Send Me', Referencing US Military's Desire to Go to Afghanistan," *Premier Christian News*, August 27, 2021, https://premierchristian.news/us /news/article/biden-quotes-isaiah-here-i-am-lord-send-me-referencing -us-military-s-desire-to-go-to-afghanistan.

9. See Andrew L. Whitehead and Samuel L. Perry, *Taking America Back for God: Christian Nationalism in the United States* (Oxford: Oxford University Press, 2020), 118.

10. Eugene Scott, "More than Half of White Evangelicals Say America's Declining White Population Is a Negative Thing," *Washington Post*, July 18, 2018, https://www.washingtonpost.com/news/the-fix/wp/2018/07 /18/more-than-half-of-white-evangelicals-say-americas-declining-white -population-is-a-negative-thing/.

11. "Immigrants are invading the homeland" is a long-standing rhetoric used by those who favor nativist politics. In recent years immigrants have been described as an "invasion" by Fox News, CNN, and MSNBC. For example, in a *Fox News* article on October 19, 2018, Newt Gingrich described a caravan of immigrants as "attempting to invade and attack the U.S." An August 4, 2019, article in *The Washington Post* said that after the 2019 El Paso shooting, there has been much debate over whether the use of immigrant invasion rhetoric by the current president of the United States had influenced the shooter, whose alleged manifesto

was entitled "Hispanic invasion of Texas"; see also "'Drug dealers, criminals, rapists': What Trump Thinks of Mexicans," *BBC*, August 31, 2016, https://www.bbc.com/news/av/world-us-canada-37230916.

12. See Tom Kertscher, "Is Black Lives Matter a Marxist Movement?," Politifact, July 21, 2020, https://www.politifact.com/article/2020/jul/21/black-lives-matter-marxist-movement/; and Kate Shellnutt, "Southern Baptists Keep Quarreling Over Critical Race Theory," *Christianity Today*, December 3, 2020, https://www.christianitytoday.com/news/2020/december/southern-baptist-critical-race-theory-debate-crt-seminary-s.html.

13. "The 1619 Project," *New York Times*, August 14, 2019, https://www.nytimes.com/interactive/2019/08/14/magazine/1619-america-slavery.html.

14. For more on the myth of "Hardworking America," see George Packer, "How America Fractured into Four Parts," *The Atlantic*, July/August 2021, https://www.theatlantic.com/magazine/archive/2021/07/george-packer-four-americas/619012/.

15. On housing discrimination, see John Wake, "The Shocking Truth 50 Years After the 1968 Fair Housing Act: The Black Homeownership Paradox," *Forbes*, May 16, 2019, https://www.forbes.com/sites/johnwake/2019/05/16/the-shocking-truth-about-the-u-s-black-homeownership-rate-50-years-after-the-1968-fair-housing-act/?sh=326f458163ba.

16. Elizabeth Dias, "'Christianity Will Have Power,'" *New York Times*, August 9, 2020, https://www.nytimes.com/2020/08/09/us/evangelicals-trump-christianity.html.

17. This statistic is based on the Electoral College vote (304 of 531). See Rob Griffin, John Halpin, and Ruy Teixeira, "Voter Trends in 2016," CAP, November 1, 2017, https://www.americanprogress.org/article/voter-trends-in-2016/.

18. Pew Research Center, "White Evangelicals See Trump as Fighting for Their Beliefs, Though Many Have Mixed Feelings About His Personal Conduct," March 12, 2020, https://www.pewforum.org/2020/03/12/white-evangelicals-see-trump-as-fighting-for-their-beliefs-though-many-have-mixed-feelings-about-his-personal-conduct/#half-of-americans-say-the-bible-should-influence-u-s-laws.

19. "8 Facts about George Washington and Religion," MountVernon.org, accessed December 3, 2021, https://www.mountvernon.org/george-washington/religion/8-facts-about-george-washington-and-religion/.

20. "Jefferson's Religious Beliefs," Monticello.org, accessed December 3,

2021, https://www.monticello.org/site/research-and-collections
/jeffersons-religious-beliefs (article courtesy of the Thomas Jefferson
Encyclopedia).

21. Historians have highlighted the fact that some of Benjamin Franklin's
actions later in life appear contradictory to his claims of being a deist
(which appear in his autobiography). See, for example, Thomas S. Kidd,
"The Complicated Religious Life of Ben Franklin," *Baylor Magazine*
(Fall 2017), https://baylor.edu/alumni/magazine/1601/index.php?id
=944746; see also John Fea, "Benjamin Franklin: Not a Deist, but Not a
Christian," *Brewminate*, January 17, 2021, http://brewminate
.com/benjamin-franklin-not-a-deist-but-not-a-christian/.

22. "September 8, 1664: New Amsterdam becomes New York," History.com,
accessed December 2, 2021, https://www.history.com/this-day-in-history
/new-amsterdam-becomes-new-york.

23. Philip Gorski, *American Covenant: A History of Civil Religion from
the Puritans to the Present* (Princeton, NJ: Princeton University Press,
2019), xiv.

CHAPTER 7: STRANGERS IN A STRANGE LAND

1. N. T. Wright, *The Challenge of Jesus: Rediscovering Who Jesus Was and Is*
(Downers Grove, IL: InterVarsity, 1999), 36–37.

2. CBS, "More Than 200 Bodies Found at Indigenous School in Canada,"
May 31, 2021, https://www.cbsnews.com/news/215-bodies-found
-canada-indigenous-school/; Paula Newton, "'Unthinkable' Discovery
in Canada as Remains of 215 Children Found Buried Near Residential
School," CNN, updated June 1, 2021, https://www.cnn.com/2021
/05/28/world/children-remains-discovered-canada-kamloops-school
/index.html.

3. Kevin J. Vanhoozer, *Faith Speaking Understanding: Performing the Drama
of Doctrine* (Louisville: Westminster John Knox, 2014), 182.

4. See Lamin Sanneh, introduction to *The Ministry of the Spirit,* by Roland
Allen (Cambridge, UK: Lutterworth Press, 2006).

5. Atossa Araxia Abrahamian, *The Cosmopolites: The Coming of the Global
Citizen* (New York: Columbia Global Reports, 2015), 114.

6. Miriam Adeney, *Kingdom Without Borders: The Untold Story of Global
Christianity* (Downers Grove, IL: InterVarsity, 2009), 275. Emphasis
added.

7. Lamin Sanneh, *Translating the Message: The Missionary Impact on Culture*,
2nd ed. (Maryknoll, NY: Orbis Books, 2009), 78.

8. Sanneh, *Translating the Message*, 251.

9. Lilias's story would likely have been lost to history had it not been for the persistent and dedicated research of Miriam Huffman Rockness, who scoured archives searching for correspondence, journals, and documents to piece together the varied tapestry of her life, portrayed in the biography *A Passion for the Impossible: The Life of Lilias Trotter* (Grand Rapids, MI: Discovery House, 2015).
10. Rockness, *A Passion for the Impossible*, 230.
11. Rockness, *A Passion for the Impossible*, 271.
12. Rockness, *A Passion for the Impossible*, 301.
13. Lesslie Newbigin, *The Open Secret: An Introduction to the Theology of Mission*, rev. ed. (Grand Rapids, MI: Eerdmans, 1995), 147.
14. Newbigin, *Open Secret*, 180.

CHAPTER 8: MY FELLOW CITIZENS

1. Salvador de Luna is my uncle in Laredo, Texas.
2. *New Samaria* is my terminology for diversity that includes immigrants; ethnic, young leaders; and other marginalized groups. See also my book, *Embracing the New Samaria: Opening Our Eyes to Our Multiethnic Future* (Colorado Springs: NavPress, 2021).
3. William H. Frey, "The US Will Become 'Minority White' in 2045, Census Projects," Brookings, March 14, 2018, https://www.brookings.edu/blog/the-avenue/2018/03/14/the-us-will-become-minority-white-in-2045-census-projects/.
4. An allusion to the challenge of Jesus in John 4:35-36 to see the reality that marginalized people are part of God's call for future church citizenship. The theology of that is encoded in Ephesians 2–4.
5. C. S. Lewis, *The Weight of Glory: Collected Letters of C. S. Lewis* (New York: HarperOne, 2001), 45–46.
6. The Hollies, "He Ain't Heavy, He's My Brother," *He Ain't Heavy, He's My Brother* © 1969 Parlophone Epic.

CHAPTER 9: POLITICS, PULPIT, AND PEW

1. "Evangelical Leaders from All 50 States Urge President Trump to Reconsider Reduction in Refugee Resettlement," World Relief, February 8, 2017, https://worldrelief.org/evangelical-leaders-from-all-50-states-urge-president-trump-to-reconsider-reduction-in-refugee-resettlment/.
2. Kaitlyn Schiess, *The Liturgy of Politics: Spiritual Formation for the Sake of Neighbor* (Downers Grove, IL: InterVarsity, 2020), 13–14.
3. Schiess, *Liturgy of Politics*, 14. Emphasis added.
4. Obery M. Hendricks, Jr., *The Politics of Jesus: Rediscovering the True*

Revolutionary Nature of Jesus' Teachings and How They Have Been Corrupted (New York: Three Leaves Press, 2006), 5.

5. N. T. Wright, *Surprised by Hope: Rethinking Heaven, the Resurrection, and the Mission of the Church* (New York: HarperCollins, 2008), 93.

6. Henricks, *Politics of Jesus*, 104.

7. Hendricks, *Politics of Jesus*, 106.

8. Walter Wink, as quoted in Hendricks, *Politics of Jesus*, 172.

9. Hendricks, *Politics of Jesus*, 118.

10. Adam L. Gustine, *Becoming a Just Church: Cultivating Communities of God's Shalom* (Downers Grove, IL: InterVarsity, 2019), 58.

11. Justo L. González, *Mañana: Christian Theology from a Hispanic Perspective* (Nashville: Abingdon, 1990).

12. Gustine, *Becoming a Just Church*, 61.

13. David Bentley Hart, *The Story of Christianity: A History of 2000 Years of the Christian Faith* (London: Quercus, 2015), 68.

14. Schiess, *Liturgy of Politics*, 62.

15. F. E. Adcock, *Roman Political Ideas and Practice* (Ann Arbor: University of Michigan Press, 1959), 76.

16. Drew G. I. Hart, *Who Will Be a Witness?: Igniting Activism for God's Justice, Love, and Deliverance* (Harrisonburg, VA: Herald Press, 2020), 177.

17. As quoted in Matt Croasmun, "Do Politics Belong in the Church?" *Christian Century*, September 24, 2018, https://www.christiancentury.org/article/opinion/do-politics-belong-church.

CHAPTER 10: IF MY PEOPLE HUMBLE THEMSELVES

1. Michael W. Smith, "Agnus Dei," *Go West Young Man* © 1990 Reunion Records.

2. Richard Rohr, "Order, Disorder, Reorder," Center for Action and Contemplation, February 23, 2016, https://cac.org/order-disorder-reorder-2016-02-23/.

3. Marva J. Dawn, *Reaching Out without Dumbing Down: A Theology of Worship for This Urgent Time* (Grand Rapids, MI: Eerdmans, 1995), 242.

4. This oath is based on the oath of allegiance taken by new US citizens (https://www.uscis.gov/citizenship/learn-about-citizenship/the-naturalization-interview-and-test/naturalization-oath-of-allegiance-to-the-united-states-of-america).

CONTRIBUTORS

TINA BOESCH has lived in seven countries on three continents. She serves as manager of the Lifeway women's Bible study publishing team and is the author of *Given: The Forgotten Meaning and Practice of Blessing* (NavPress).

JULIET LIU is the pastor of Life on the Vine, a church in a northwest suburb of Chicago. She has also served with InterVarsity Christian Fellowship, Northshore Chinese Christian Church, and at Trinity International University, and is chair of the board and writing team member for Missio Alliance.

ALEJANDRO MANDES is a disciple maker, church planter, and cultural adventurer with initiatives including Immigrant Hope and the EFCA GATEWAY Theological Institute. He serves on the board of directors for the Immigration Alliance and the National Association of Evangelicals.

SEAN PALMER is the teaching pastor at Ecclesia Houston and the author of *Speaking by the Numbers: Enneagram Wisdom for Teachers, Pastors, and Communicators* (IVP) and *Unarmed Empire: In Search of Beloved Community* (Cascade).

MICHELLE AMI REYES is vice president of the Asian American Christian Collaborative and co-executive director of Pax. She is also the scholar in residence at Hope Community Church and author of *Becoming All Things: How Small Changes Lead to Lasting Connections Across Cultures* (Zondervan).

MANDY SMITH is a native of Australia and is a pastor and the author of *The Vulnerable Pastor: How Human Limitations Empower Our Ministry* (IVP) and *Unfettered: Imagining a Childlike Faith Beyond the Baggage of Western Culture* (Brazos).

RYAN TAFILOWSKI is an instructor at Denver Seminary, where he teaches theology and the history of Christianity, and pastor of Foothills Fellowship Church in Littleton, Colorado.

DEREK VREELAND is the author of several books, including *By the Way: Getting Serious About Following Jesus* (Herald Press). He is currently the discipleship pastor at Word of Life Church in Saint Joseph, Missouri.

ANGIE WARD is a teacher and author with nearly thirty years of ministry-leadership experience. She is the general editor of the Kingdom Conversations series and author of *I Am a Leader: When Women Discover the Joy of Their Calling* (both NavPress). She serves as assistant director of the Doctor of Ministry program at Denver Seminary.

KAREN WILK works with Resonate Global Mission and Forge Canada, teaching, coaching, and practicing what it means to discover and join the Spirit on God's mission in our neighborhoods. She also enjoys being a spouse, mom, local pastor, and neighbor.

ROD WILSON has served as psychologist, pastor, educator, writer, and consultant, including fifteen years as president of Regent College in Vancouver, Canada. His abiding focus is on how the spiritual and human dimensions of life impact each other.

ABOUT KINGDOM CONVERSATIONS

To be a Christian is to be conscious of and responsive to three realities at once: the past, where we see that God has spoken and intervened to bless his people to be a blessing; the future, with confidence that God will involve us in his coming resolution of the world's pain and suffering; and the present, where we live, and move, and have our being.

When we step back to consider the vantage point of our good God, who is the same yesterday, today, and forever, we find our footing and our way of glorifying God in our time.

In the Kingdom Conversations series we dare to consider that any issue, no matter how complex, may be brought into conversation with what we know of God and of history and of one another.

They are "conversations" because they gather the perspectives of various Christian leaders to consider the question together.

They are "Kingdom" because they are each submitted in humility and hope to God, trusting that God himself will lead us into all truth.

ABOUT MISSIO ALLIANCE

THE CHURCH IS KNOWN FOR MANY THINGS, but not always for looking like Jesus. The world desperately needs individuals and communities whose lives testify to the transformative power of Christ's life, death, and resurrection. Missio Alliance exists to resource, gather, and embolden Christians to reshape the church's witness in the world.

Rooted in the global, biblical convictions and calls to action of the Cape Town Commitment, the ministry of Missio Alliance is animated by a strong and distinctive theological identity that emphasizes:

Comprehensive Mutuality: Advancing the partnered voice and leadership of women and men among the beautiful diversity of the body of Christ across race, culture, and theological heritage.

Hopeful Witness: Advancing a way of being the people of God in the world that reflects an unwavering and joyful hope in the lordship of Christ in the church and over all things.

Church in Mission: Advancing a vision of the local church in which our identity and testimony is found and expressed through our active participation in God's mission in the world.

To explore our growing library of resources, visit missioalliance.org.

NavPress is the book-publishing arm of The Navigators.

Since 1933, The Navigators has helped people around the world bring hope and purpose to others in college campuses, local churches, workplaces, neighborhoods, and hard-to-reach places all over the world, face-to-face and person-by-person in an approach we call Life-to-Life® discipleship. We have committed together to know Christ, make Him known, and help others do the same.®

Would you like to join this adventure of discipleship and disciplemaking?

- Take a Digital Discipleship Journey at **navigators.org/disciplemaking**.
- Get more discipleship and disciplemaking content at **thedisciplemaker.org**.
- Find your next book, Bible, or discipleship resource at **navpress.com**.

CP1790